The 8 Superpowers of Successful Entrepreneurs

The 8 Superpowers of Successful Entrepreneurs

From Zero to Hero: The Business Strategies Adopted by Global Icons

Marina Nicholas

BEP

BUSINESS EXPERT PRESS

Leader in applied, concise business books

First published in 2021 by
Business Expert Press, LLC
222 East 46th Street, New York, NY 10017
www.businessexpertpress.com

ISBN-13: 978-1-63742-000-3 (paperback)
ISBN-13: 978-1-63742-001-0 (e-book)

Business Expert Press Entrepreneurship and Small Business Management Collection

Collection ISSN: 1946-5653 (print)
Collection ISSN: 1946-5661 (electronic)

First edition: 2021

10 9 8 7 6 5 4 3 2 1

Dedicated to my wonderful son, Bruno

Author's royalties donated to Pencils of Promise.

A non-profit organization that builds schools and increases educational opportunities in the developing world. Pencils of Promise believe where you start in life shouldn't dictate where you finish.

https://pencilsofpromise.org/

Description

THESE STRATEGIES WILL GIVE YOU SUPERPOWERS

Many books have been written about the high-performance habits successful entrepreneurs adopt, from their daily meditation to how they lead their teams. For Marina Nicholas, her fascination was more about their entrepreneurial journey.

1. *From Zero:* When starting a business, what strategies did they adopt to overcome the odds?
2. *To Hero:* As a highly successful entrepreneur, how did they use their wealth to help humanity and the planet?

After years of extensive research, Marina discovered that just eight strategies were adopted by billionaire entrepreneurs.

PROBLEM—PERSEVERANCE—POSITIONING—PROXIMITY— PEOPLE—PARTNERSHIPS—PROCESS—PLANET

Whether you enjoy inspirational stories or seek to discover your superpower, the strategies and exercises in this book will help you. Each of the eight strategies is illustrated by real case studies.

Over 25 case studies like these:

- A white trouser problem led to a billion-dollar empire
- The invention of a passionate surfer leads to sales of 35 million cameras
- A 7-year journey of poverty and rejection led to a $500 million franchise
- A happy tribe built a $1.2 billion company
- A monk builds a tribe of 35 million followers within 4 years
- A village visit resulted in 100 million pairs of shoes gifted

Keywords

entrepreneurism; social entrepreneurs; growth strategy; impact entrepreneurs; small business management; social sustainability; start up; leadership; visionary; millionaire mindset

Contents

Testimonials

"A timely publication for a post COVID19 world and for the new greener and socially orientated entrepreneurs seeking to make an impact." **—Dr Dane Anderton, Alliance Manchester Business School, Manchester University**

"Wow. What an uplifting and action-orientated must-read for Entrepreneurs for our times. If you want to lead now and build for the future, then read this easy to digest and learn from work by Marina Nicholas. An uplifting and inspirational book on how to be a successful Entrepreneur and Leader and build a great business to grow and sustain society" **—Professor Phil Harris, Executive Director, University of Chester Business Research Institute**

"A must-read book for entrepreneurs looking to understand and unlock the "superpowers" of some of the most successful entrepreneurs in recent history. Refreshingly, Marina recognizes the power of being socially aware within these strategies which are unpacked through a range of inspirational case studies, practical tips and invaluable self-reflection points." **—Sarah Trouten, CEO, Institute of Enterprise and Entrepreneurs**

"The essence of the iconic journey of global entrepreneurs is captured in eight success mantras by Marina in her inspiring book. The work is so current and relevant, leaving atrial for those inclined towards entrepreneurship to realise their self-worth and later for the philanthropic reach out to society. Local and global perspectives shared through case citings are lucid and truly remarkable." **—Professor Biju Toms, Director, Professional Studies, Christ University, Bangalore**

"Using an easy going and accessible style, Marina draws on her vast experience in leading and advising businesses to identify, what she calls, the eight most significant success strategies for entrepreneurs. A very relevant and timely publication that draws easy to understand narratives from the profiles of some of

the World's most high-profile entrepreneurs to shed light, both on the distinct opportunities that surround each of us and on the entrepreneurial process. This book contains invaluable case-material, shaped into a simple and novel structure, that stimulates entrepreneurial thinking and gives insight into the paths to entrepreneurial success." —**David W. Taylor, Principal Lecturer in Entrepreneurship, Manchester Metropolitan University and Honorary Fellow of the Institute of Enterprise and Entrepreneurs.**

"The publication tackles on a wide range of topics applicable to everyday entrepreneurial pursuits but also including 'place' and 'plant', two key components that are increasingly gaining attention across the policy and practitioner world. Light is shed on the role of entrepreneurial ecosystems and how each one is different, further emphasising the role of 'place' in strategy and value capture. A timely publication for a post COVID19 world and for the new greener and socially orientated entrepreneurs seeking to make an impact". —**Dr Dane Anderton, Director of Programmes in Executive Education and Senior Lecture in Strategy and Innovation, Alliance Manchester Business School, Manchester University**

My Story

Successful entrepreneurs. How do they launch their ideas to the forefront of a crowded market? How do they discover the needle-in-a-haystack route to overwhelmingly exceed all of their goals and drive toward immense success? And most importantly, what do all their stories have in common? For decades, these have been the questions I have been asking myself. My journey toward the answers started when I was a 19 year old University graduate, I read my first autobiography, Anita Roddick's "Body and Soul," about her journey building the Body Shop. Still seeking to accumulate more knowledge, the next book I devoured was Richard Branson's "Like A Virgin." Their entrepreneurial journey's building businesses from zero to hero inspired me to research, learn, and experiment.

At 24 years old, I had my first experience. I was approached by a company to build a 60-seater telemarketing business within 3 months. At that time, I was in a secure salaried position heading a telemarketing unit. The prospect of venturing on my own excited me, so I took the leap and handed in my notice, throwing myself into a career as a self-employed consultant building businesses.

I remember walking into the empty floor of the building and the CEO saying here it is, "let's build it." I was part of a team of four with the brief to hire sixty people, create the operating framework, and start generating sales, all within twelve weeks. It was a fabulous opportunity that ignited my passion for building a business from zero to hero.

Having now worked for over three decades, I look at my career as having three distinct acts, like a play. In my first act, I was primarily a DOER, acting as a consultant helping build businesses.

In my second act, I discovered the joy of being a WRITER. Just after I got married, I was given a 5% chance of having a baby by doctors. This led to a seven year quest to achieve my dream of becoming a mother. After testing most complementary and conventional medicines, my beautiful son was born against all the odds. Being asked by many couples "how did you do it?," I was inspired to write the medical strategies I adopted in a book. *3 Steps to Fertility - A Couple's Guide to Maximising Their Ability to Conceive*, was published in six languages and continues to help couples globally achieve their dream of parenthood.

During this second act, I suffered a near death experience. Grateful for a second chance at life, I decided to focus my efforts on small to medium sized businesses (SME) who are passionate about doing business for good. I felt I could make a greater impact faster and try to address the issue that only 1 in 5 entrepreneurs successfully reaches five years in business.

Today I am enjoying my third act as a TEACHER. Coaching, mentoring, advising, and teaching business strategies to SMEs and large enterprises. I am thrilled that I can now combine all three acts and be a DOER, WRITER, and TEACHER.

This book is a culmination of years of research into the business strategies of highly successful entrepreneurs. Rather than be a teacher who recites business strategies and theories to people, I am keen to validate anything I coach, teach, or advise. I have personally tried and tested business strategies on my own projects as well as with my clients over the years. Some strategies I tried have failed, until I discovered the eight strategies adopted by billionaires. I affectionately call them the "8 SUPERPOWERS."

In the last decade, I have implemented the eight superpower strategies which has led to seven awards, ranging from International Business Woman of the Year to an award for the most "Innovative Product" selected from eighty global entrants, in a sector I had no experience. While these accolades are pleasing, I am driven by how I can add value to people's lives and make a difference.

My goal with this book is to make a difference and pay it forward: Harnessing the Power of the Planet, being a impact entrepreneur. The royalties from my medical book enabled children in Nepal and Kenya to benefit from education. With your help, I aspire to build a whole school, through Pencils of Promise, a non-profit organization that builds schools and increases educational opportunities in the developing world, from the royalties from books and courses. This is a value that I embrace and showcase throughout this book; a compilation of zero to hero stories of successful entrepreneurs who now pay it forward.

I am grateful to the entrepreneurs in this book for being my mentors. Researching the strategies of how you went from zero to hero has inspired me to learn, experiment, implement, fail, or succeed and try again. I am also grateful to you, the readers of this book. You have taken valuable time out of your day to read this book. You are here for a reason. You have picked this book today as you have a calling to discover your entrepreneurial superpower. Join me on a voyage of discovery.

Marina

Acknowledgments

I would like to thank Bruno, my son, for his wonderful support every day. You light up my world in every way and motivate me to try my best. Thank you for spending your school summer holiday editing this book. Your mastery of the English language, storytelling and grammar is way beyond your years.

Writing a book during pandemic times really brought home what is important to me. I could not have written this book without the love and support of my wonderful family and friends. The world around us has been volatile and uncertain, but you motivated me to keep going when it was a struggle.

Thank you to all the inspirational people featured in this book. It has been an absolute joy to follow your journey from zero to hero. You truly are the world's greatest mentors paving the way for a generation of impact entrepreneurs.

A thank you to Nick Hexter for his creative genius in bringing the 8 Superpowers images to life and designing an eye-catching book cover.

Thank you to the team at Business Expert Press for believing in me. I wanted to write a book that if my 20-year-old self had read it I may have discovered my superpower earlier and made a greater impact in the world. Thank you for allowing me to be creative and for bringing it to life.

Thank you to my clients worldwide for giving me the opportunity to implement my 8 P Method in your business. For putting your trust in me to grow your business and for teaching me so much. Without you I would not have been able to make an impact on so many people globally.

Finally, thank you to you, the reader. If you are familiar with my work, you will know that I am grateful for this second chance at life after a near death experience. Every day is a blessing to connect and be of service to others. I truly believe that each one of us has a superpower. Thank you for allowing me to take you on a journey of discovery. Together we are making a difference to humanity and the planet.

Introduction

We are living in the era of the Fourth Industrial Revolution, where how we live, work, and relate to one another has fundamentally changed. An era where technology is embedded within societies and the relationship between man and machine has never been so intertwined.

INDUSTRIAL REVOLUTION
TRANSFORMING INDUSTRIES AND INNOVATION

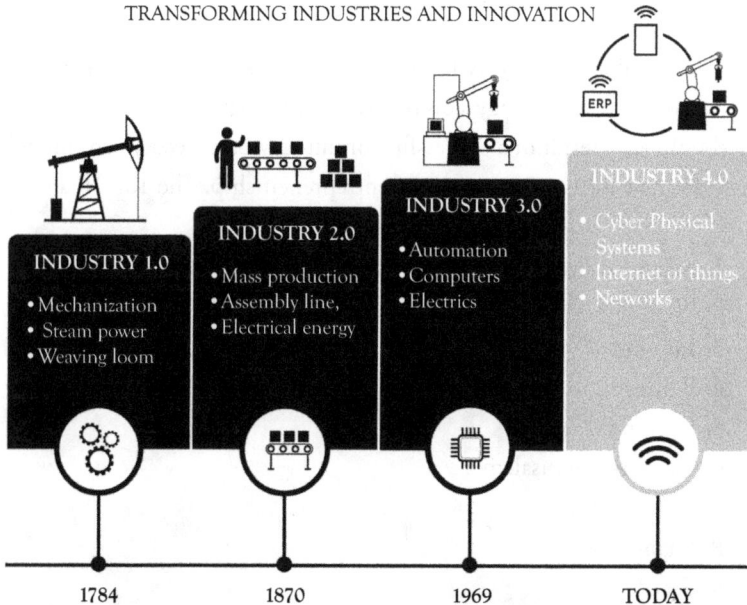

INDUSTRY 1.0
- Mechanization
- Steam power
- Weaving loom

INDUSTRY 2.0
- Mass production
- Assembly line,
- Electrical energy

INDUSTRY 3.0
- Automation
- Computers
- Electrics

INDUSTRY 4.0
- Cyber Physical Systems
- Internet of things
- Networks

| 1784 | 1870 | 1969 | TODAY |

In 2008, Microsoft featured as one of the largest companies in the world and it was the only technology based company. Today, seven out of the top 10 are technology led, according to the Global Startup Ecosystem Report. We have shifted from the Third Revolution, which began in the 1950s, with advances in digital systems, communication, and computer power enabling the processing and sharing of information, to the Fourth Industrial Revolution, which has resulted in the rise of entrepreneurism.

The advances of the Third Revolution has enabled increased connectivity around the globe making it easier for people to set up a business. Today, you can raise funds within a day, recruit talent from anywhere in the world, download business processing tools that improve efficiency and promote your business to millions across social media platforms. This is why the global start up economy has seen a rise of 20% from 2017 and is worth nearly $3 trillion. That's the size of a not-so-small economy, larger than the Gross Domestic Product (GDP) of the United Kingdom, France, or Brazil.

The Rise of the Entrepreneur

Silicon Valley is heralded as the first startup ecosystem where entrepreneurs, investors, and talent became aware of their commonality to build businesses and think and act as a community, sharing knowledge, and resources; a hive mind mentality.

Today, Silicon Valley is home to thousands of startups as well as the world's top technology companies, like Google, Apple, Cisco, and Facebook. As a result of a successful community based ecosystem model, there are now 270 global centers of entrepreneurship. The Top 10 are:

1. Silicon Valley
2. New York City
3. London
4. Beijing
5. Boston
6. Tel Aviv—Jerusalem
7. Los Angeles
8. Shanghai
9. Seattle
10. Stockholm

This ranking, assessed by StartUp Genome, is driven by one question. Which ecosystem will an early stage startup have the best chance of having global success? The ranking looks at key factors such as the number of exits over $50 million, market reach, connectedness, talent, and knowledge.

Ecosystem Value is a measure capturing the value of startups funded and exited in an ecosystem over two and half years. In number one position is Silicon Valley with an ecosystem value of $677 billion (global average is $10.5 billion) and the total early stage funding at $18 billion (global avg.

$431 million). New York City is $147 billion with early stage funding at $8.3 billion, then London at $92 billion with total early stage funding at $6 billion. Compare this to an ecosystem ranked 20th, Seoul, which has $1 billion early stage funding and $39 billion ecosystem value. It is easy to see why the location that an entrepreneur chooses to build a business is crucial.

Today, more than 80 ecosystems globally have produced a billion-dollar startup
When term was popularized on 2013, only 4 ecosystems produced unicorns or billion-dollar exits
Ecosystems with Billion-Dollar Club Startups (Unicorns or exits), 2013-2019

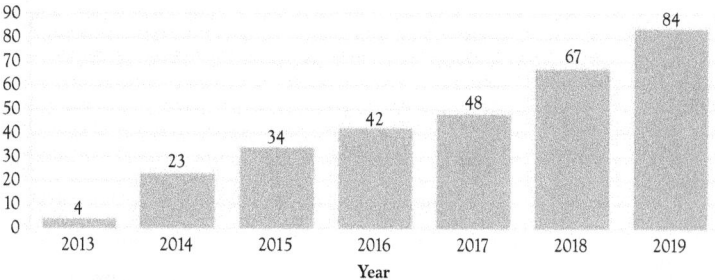

Startup ecosystems are an important driver of economic growth. London and New York City ecosystems emerged following the 2007–2009 Great Recession—in an attempt to diversify from reliance on traditional strengths in finance. Today, the Asia Pacific region is demonstrating the fastest growth among all the continents.

Percent of Ecosystems from Continent among Top Global Ecosystems
● Asia–Pacific ● Europe ● North America ● South America

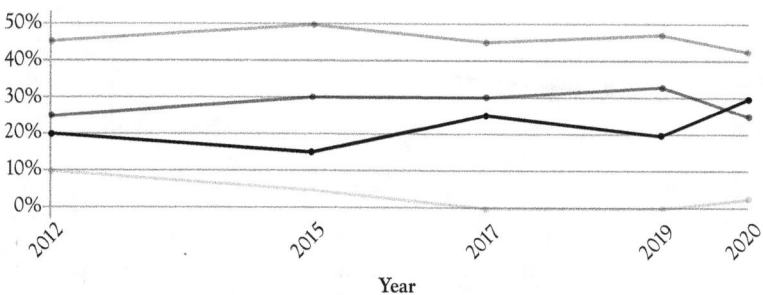

As a result of growing ecosystems, the rise of the entrepreneur is evident. There are 472 million entrepreneurs worldwide, 305 million total startups annually with 100 million opening each year. 1.35 million are tech startups, 3,173 companies accelerated from 185 accelerator programs and 182 exits (of companies accelerated). With female founded startups around the world landing a record 4,399 investments in 2019, according to data from All Raise.

The Covid-19 Ripple Effect

It would be remiss of me to not highlight the scenario in the present moment as I write this book. An unprecedented event occurred in the first quarter of 2020, a virus pandemic paralyzed the world socially and economically. Like an earthquake, the ripple effect tore through the global startup ecosystem resulting in two significant effects, capital challenges and demand drop.

1. Capital Challenges

4 out of 10 startups had less than 3 months' capital, meaning collapse would be inevitable unless they fundraise or demand kicks in. Classed as a "fundraising fiasco" as 3 out of 4 startups had their fundraising process disrupted. 18% of startups with term sheets had a funding round cancelled by investors and 54% experienced a funding round delay.

4 out of every 10 startups today are in the "red zone", up 29% since Dec. 2019
This means they have 3 months or fewer of capital runway
African (56%) and South American (44%) startups are in the most trouble, while Oceanian (31%) and European (35%) startups are doing relatively better

South American   Oceania   North America   Europe   Asia   Africa   Global Avg

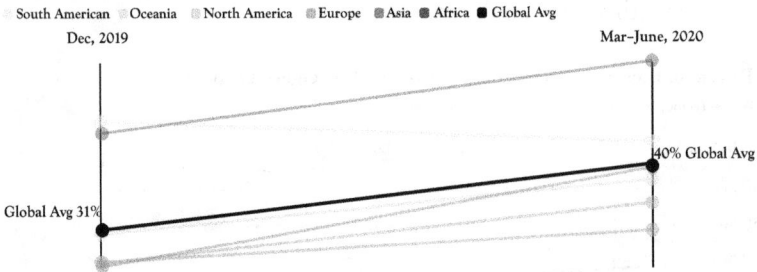

2. Demand Drop

72% startups experienced a drop in revenue since the crisis hit, with an average experiencing a 32% decline. According to the Startup Genome Covid-19 Impact Insights report, 10% expect revenues to grow, 40% expect to stay the same, and 28% predict a drop in revenue over the coming years. 60% have laid off employees or reduced salaries. The main jobs to suffer are 36% direct sales, 29% marketing, 31% research and development, and 32% with product roles. 71% of startups have reduced expenses by an average of 22%.

This is a Recession coupled with an acceleration into the digital economy. The 4th Revolution on steroids!

Winners and Losers

With the human population mobilized and daily lives disrupted, it is undoubtedly the worst economic downturn since 1929. The pandemic has accelerated the demise of companies that were already in trouble and the bankruptcy announcements across industries will continue over the coming years. The automotive, aviation, retail, oil, and gas sectors being the hardest hit. Well-known brands like Hertz, Latam Airlines, JCPenney, Neiman Marcus, and Whiting Petroleum have all filed for bankruptcy within six months of the pandemic. Daily announcements of companies laying off people and closing their doors is becoming the new normal.

However, every crisis creates opportunity. History tells us that 50% of the Fortune 500 companies started during a recession. Companies like Facebook, LinkedIn, and Dropbox. During Lockdown times, the dependency on digital and technology products accelerated as humans desire to continue behaviors like shopping, entertainment, and socializing. Covid-19 accelerated the growth of tech companies like Zoom, Slack, and Spotify. As demand for online shopping skyrocketed, Amazon boss, Jeff Bezos saw his fortune grow by $31 billion and is predicted to be the world's first trillionaire by 2026. Overnight, online conferencing company Zoom became a remote working essential, a multi-generational connection tool, and a household name. Zoom Founder, Eric Yuan enjoyed a 140% rise in his fortune to $8.5 billion. In the 2020 Top 10 Billionaires Index, eight people are in technology.

Like the dinosaur era, we are experiencing an extinction event with millions of companies, from large corporations to startups, are in survival mode. It truly is an era of the *"survival of the fittest."* As Charles Darwin said 150 years ago in 1869, *"It is not the strongest or the most intelligent who will survive but those who can best manage change."*

Success Matters

In order to navigate the long term ripple effect of Covid-19, two factors are critical to an entrepreneur's success.

1. **The Ecosystem**

The property development adage, "location, location, location" is also true for Startups. Immersion into an ecosystem with like-minded people passionate about innovation, growth, and scale is a proven success model. Chapter 4 dives into the Power of Proximity in detail.

2. **The Strategies**

While the WHERE to be in business is important, the focus of this book is on the HOW. You can have hundreds of entrepreneurs in the same ecosystem, yet only one may achieve Unicorn status. Entrepreneurism can be likened to the '4 minute mile' analogy. In 1964, Roger Bannister broke the 4 minute mile barrier that had stood for decades. Within a year, another four people broke the record after seeing it was possible. Since then, over 1,000 runners have adopted the high performance strategies to complete a 4-minute mile.

In entrepreneurial terms, in the 1900s, a century ago, a *billionaire* individual did not exist. Fast forward to today, there are 46.8 million millionaires with a combined wealth of $158.3 trillion. Of which, 2,825 have risen to billionaire status, according to Wealth-X. Millionaires now have about half the total global wealth. In 2019, the number of millionaires rose by 1.1 million in one year alone globally.

As a result, new terms to describe the levels of entrepreneurial achievement have emerged. A "Unicorn" is a business with $1 billion to $10 billion turnover. "Decacorns" have $10 billion to $50 billion turnover and "Titans" $50 billion plus. Let's put that into perspective.

- 1 second is 1 second
- 1 million seconds is 12 days (a vacation)
- 1 billion seconds is 30 years (a career)
- 50 billion is 1,500 years (a human lifetime plus some)
- a trillion is 30,000 years (longer than human civilization)

It's about understanding the scale to truly appreciate entrepreneurs who have scaled these heights. Once we have this scale, entrepreneurs who have built companies from zero to hero inspire us to learn HOW. Many books have been written about the high performance habits successful entrepreneurs adopt, from their daily meditation techniques and fitness routines to how they lead their teams. I have always been more fascinated about their journey from zero to hero.

- *From Zero:* When starting a business, what strategies did they adopt to overcome the odds?
- *To Hero:* As a highly successful entrepreneur, how did they use their wealth to help humanity and the planet?

What is an Entrepreneur?

According to the Oxford Dictionary, the definition of an entrepreneur is *"someone who sets up a business taking on financial risks in the hope of profit."* Let's look at the definition from an entrepreneur's perspective.

Entrepreneurship is living a few years of your life like most people won't so that you can spend the rest of your life like most people can't.

—Anon.

Being an entrepreneur isn't just a job title, and it isn't about starting a company. It's a state of mind. It's about seeing connections others can't, seizing opportunities others won't, and forging new directions that others haven't.

—Tony Birch.

Being an entrepreneur is sexy for those who haven't done it. In reality it's grotty, tough work where you will be filled with self doubt. Entrepreneurs are survivors.

—Mark Suster, American Venture Capitalist.

Entrepreneurship is about turning what excites you in life into capital, so that you can do more of it and move forward with it.

—Richard Branson, Virgin Group.

Entrepreneurship is not only a mindset but a skillset.

—Mitchell Kapor, one of the pioneers of the personal computing industry.

The Superhero Selection Criteria

There are millions of entrepreneurs globally, so how do you select ones to feature in a book about success strategies? Entrepreneurs were required to meet two criteria.

Criteria #1: Zero to Hero

Millions of talented people lead companies in roles such as Chief Executive Officer (CEO) and Managing Director (MD). Whilst they are great captains of the boat steering it to success, they did not invent the boat. This book only features entrepreneurs, not leaders of companies, who demonstrated they adopted a superpower strategy to create, build, and launch a new product or service thereby achieving global success.

Criteria #2: Philanthropic values

While showcasing the zero to hero stories and the strategies adopted by successful entrepreneurs is inspirational and educational, for me, discovering how they distribute their wealth through philanthropic endeavors to help humanity and the planet, remains at the heart of this book.

Societal expectations of "giving back" have risen, regardless of whether you are rich or poor. From small acts of daily kindness and charity runs to championing front line workers during Covid, human consciousness has been raised. Only entrepreneurs with a demonstrable philanthropic track record of redistributing their wealth are featured in this book.

> *Giving is not just about making a donation. It is about making a difference.*
> —Kathy Calvin, CEO & President of the United
> Nations Foundation

> *If you're in the luckiest 1% of humanity, you owe it to the rest of humanity to think about the other 99%.*
> —Warren Buffet

We make a living by what we get, but we make a life by what we give.

—Winston Churchill

Only a life lived for others is a life worthwhile.

—Albert Einstein

Life's most persistent and urgent question is, 'What are you doing for others?'

—Martin Luther King Jr.

Categorization

With the selection criteria applied and the entrepreneurs shortlisted to feature in this book, the next phase was to categorize the entrepreneurs into industrial revolution, sector and strategy.

Table I.1 By industrial revolution

Second (1870–1950) The Age of Science and Mass Production	Third (1950–2011) The Digital Revolution	Fourth (2011 onwards) Technological Revolution

Sam Walton
Warren Buffet
	Sara Blakely
	Brian Chesky and
	    Joe Gibbin
	Steve Chen and
	    Chad Hurley
	Nick Woodman
	James Dyson
	J.K Rowling
	Bill Gates
	Tony Robbins
	Tony Hsieh
	Richard Branson
	Bernie Ecclestone
	Judith Faulkner
	Reed Hastings
	Steve Jobs
	Anita Roddick
	Muhammed Yanus
	Blake Mycoskie
		Jay Shetty
		Anne Boden
		Nikolay Storonsky and Vlad
		    Yatsenko
		Sean Rad

Table I.2 By sector

Personal Development	Finance	IT	Media
Tony Robbins Jay Shetty Sean Rad	Warren Buffet Anne Boden Nikolay Storonsky Muhammed Yanus	Bill Gates Judith Faulkner	J.K Rowling Reed Hastings Steve Chen and Chad Hurley Reed Hastings
Manufacturing/ Retail	**Hospitality**	**Sport**	**Multiple sectors**
Sara Blakely Nick Woodman James Dyson Sam Walton Tony Hsieh Steve Jobs Anita Roddick Blake Mycoskie	Brian Chesky and Joe Gibbin	Bernie Ecclestone	Richard Branson

Table I.3 By superpower strategy

PURPOSE	PRODUCT	POSITIONING	PROXIMITY
Sara Blakely Brian Chesky and Joe Gibbin Chad Hurley Nick Woodman	James Dyson J.K. Rowling	Sam Walton Bill Gates	Sean Rad
PEOPLE	**PARTNERSHIPS**	**PROCESS**	**PLANET**
Tony Robbins Warren Buffet Nick Swinmurn Jay Shetty	Richard Branson Bernie Eccelstone	Judith Faulkner Reed Hastings Anne Boden Nikolay Storonsky	Anita Roddick Muhammed Yunus Blake Mycoskie

What do I Mean by a Superpower?

A curious mind asks a curious question, "How did they do it?" To me, a Superpower is a trait, characteristic, or strategy adopted that uniquely sets them apart from the norm to succeed. A Superpower is the primary reason they overcame the odds and became a success.

How to Use This Book

This book was written such that you can either read the book in sequence or dive into a Superpower or an entrepreneur's story that appeals to you. Either way works.

The Categories

The book is split into categories, the 5 M's, in which the superpower strategies, the 8 P's, fall.

Category 1—MINDSET—Problem and Perseverance

Category 2—MARKETING—Positioning and Proximity

Category 3—MASSES—People and Partnerships

Category 4—METHOD—Process

Category 5—MOVEMENT—Planet

The Mantras

Before diving into the book, read the following entrepreneur mantras and instinctively choose the mantra that *feels* like you. Which one are you drawn to most?

"I'm driven to create something new to solve the problem"

"I will keep trying until I succeed"

"I will boldly go where no-one has been before"

"Right people, right place"

"I will create a tribe to succeed"

"Let's collaborate"

"Let's simplify"

"Be the change you want to see in the world"

Each mantra relates to one of the 8 superpowers. The one you are drawn to is likely to be your underlying superpower.

The Exercises

If you wish to evolve your superpower further, the exercises at the end of each chapter will guide you. Chapter 9 brings the 8 superpower strategies together under the 8 P framework. Why just tap into one superpower to succeed? What would happen if you adopted all 8 strategies to your business simultaneously?

Contribution

Before we get started, I would like to invite all readers to take part in this journey together by embodying the two superpower criteria from the outset. This book will provide you with the first criteria, the strategies, and tools to accelerate your success. Only you can proactively embrace the second criteria of philanthropy. By helping humanity, even in a small way, you are stepping into the persona of a superhero entrepreneur.

There are two ways to contribute:

1. *Inspire others*

   Many business books become outdated when they rely on case studies to support their methods. People and companies get profiled all the time and even as I write this book, companies are rising and falling. This is why I founded the Impact Community to remain current and champion the entrepreneurs of today who make the impossible, possible. Entrepreneurs who are not only surviving, but thriving during challenging times. If you are passionate about making an impact, please join the Impact Community. It's free. We share stories and strategies to inspire others. We believe in the POSSIBLE! Please visit www.8superpower.co
   "To be inspired is great, but to inspire others is incredible."

2. *Educate others*

   The superhero entrepreneurs in this book were selected not only for their business success but also for their philanthropic endeavors. I know this book is in your hands for a reason. If you would like to help educate those less fortunate, donations made by readers will be channeled toward Pencils of Promise. A non-profit organization that builds schools and increases educational opportunities in the developing world. https://pencilsofpromise.org/

250 million children of primary school age lack basic reading, writing, and math skills. To date, Pencils of Promise have built 531 schools, supported 2,151 teachers and impacted 110,380 students in the poorest regions of the world. To build a classroom requires $10,000, to build an entire school $50,000. My ambitious goal is to build an entire school.

Join the 8 Superpower Tribe in making this happen. Either donate or generate.

- Donate—donations gratefully received at www.8superpower.co
- Generate—recommend this book to someone else. Pay it forward. Promote the book on social media. Book sales generate royalties. All royalties from this book will be donated to Pencils of Promise.

Pencils of Promise believe where you start in life shouldn't dictate where you finish.

Education is the most powerful weapon which you can use to change the world.

—Nelson Mandela

CATEGORY I
Mindset

CHAPTER 1

Power of Problem

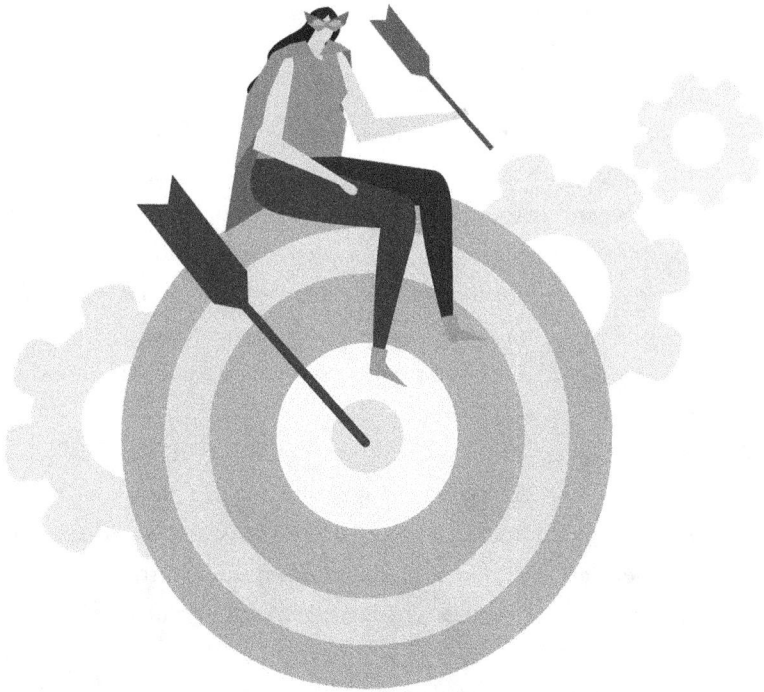

Solving Problems

Entrepreneurs with a problem solving mindset are driven to create solutions. Products are used daily that trigger thoughts like "*this would be better if....*" and "*if only this was faster...,*" yet the majority of us accept the status quo. There are a minority who decide to take action, create and launch a new product. What drives these entrepreneurs? Do they have a unique outlook and approach?

There are several approaches to problem solving.

1. **Algorithms**

   Algorithms simplify the complex by using step-by-step instructions that will produce the same result every time they are performed. The earliest algorithm recorded was in the Babylonian times, 1600 BC, on a clay tablet, an early form of an instruction manual to solve a class of problems. Today, the most famous publicized algorithm is PageRank, Google's algorithm to rank the pages on the search engine, created by Larry Page and Sergey Brin while studying at Stanford University.

2. **Heuristics**

   Heuristics, derived from Greek word meaning "to discover," uses shortcuts to produce good-enough solutions in a given timeframe. They enable quick decisions particularly when working with complex data. You may solve the problem through trial and error, having an educated guess or using rule of thumb thinking.

3. **Insights**

   Defined as the moment of sudden comprehension of a problem and the solution is often accompanied by an aha experience (Ollinger et al. 2013). Researchers say that an insight occurs because you realize that the problem is actually similar to something you have dealt with in the past. In most cases, the underlying mental processes that lead to insight happen outside of awareness.

   In the field of cognitive psychology, studies show that intuition and insight problem solving are intertwined. Intuition is an unconscious process, which provides a gut feeling or hunch for the situation. Often called the "Eureka Moment" as the solution presents itself suddenly and unexpectedly.

Studies assessing brain activity during insights show increased activity in the right side of the brain compared to problem solving not requiring insights. Many studies have shown that unconscious problem processing may take place while a person is asleep and the solution presents itself in a dream or upon awakening. Some of the world's most celebrated artists, scientists, athletes and inventors had their eureka moment during sleep.

- Chemist Dmitri Mendeleev spent 10 years trying to create a pattern that connected the chemical elements together. It was in 1869, the inspiration for the Periodic Table came to him. Writing in his diary, Medeleev said, "I saw in a dream a table where all the elements fell into place as required. Awakening, I immediately wrote it down on a piece of paper."

- One of the greatest golfers of all time, Jack Nicklaus struggled to understand why his game was below par until a new grip and golf swing came to him in a dream. Jack has won 117 golf tournaments and 18 major championships over his career.

- Film director James Cameron created both The Terminator and Avatar during dream states. The Terminator franchise has generated over $3 billion in revenue and Avatar remains the highest grossing movie with $2 billion in revenue. Not bad for a dream!

Regardless of which method the entrepreneurs featured in this chapter adopted, the common characteristic they share is a problem solving mindset. This is their superpower.

The Mantra
"I'm driven to create something new to solve the problem."

Don't be intimidated by what you don't know. That can be your greatest strength and ensure that you do things differently from everyone else.
—Sara Blakely, SPANX

When you start a company, it's more than an art than a science because it's totally unknown. Instead of solving high-profile problems, try to solve something that's deeply personal to you. Ideally, if you're an ordinary person and you've just solved your problem, you might have solved the problem for millions of people.

—Brian Chesky, Airbnb.

A really important thing when you come up with a concept is that you solve a pervasive problem for people, and you don't try to create a new way to do something that isn't necessarily broken.

—Nick Woodman, GOPRO

Someone has an itch for a problem and that they're annoyed enough to actually go out and seek a solution for it.

—Daniel Ek, Spotify

BRIAN CHESKY, JOE GEBBIA, and NATHAN BLECHARCZYK, AIRBNB
Not being able to pay the rent led to a $10 billion dollar company

In 2008, Brian, Joe, and Nathan decided to rent out three air mattresses in their San Francisco loft apartment to help pay the rent. They noticed that all the hotels in town were fully booked for the design trade show; accommodation was scarce. The flatmates successfully rented out three air mattresses with breakfast for $80 each. This led them to think—what if we could find more places to rent out? This initial success provided Brian and Joe with the momentum to explore if they were onto something.

Shortly afterwards, they successfully raised $30,000 initial investment but, to their dismay, they found that sales weren't increasing. After reviewing the website, they realized the photos were not that appealing to customers. The Founders embarked on improving the quality by visiting each listed house door to door themselves. They had successfully eliminated the source of their problem, and with a higher quality online rental website, sales doubled within a week. This growth continued and in 2011, Airbnb celebrated taking its one millionth booking. In 2012, the business doubled in a 5 month period to achieve its ten millionth booking.

Where are They Today?

Airbnb offers over 5 million places to stay, employs 13,000 people, and operates in 191 countries. Airbnb has hosted over 400 million guests since its launch. What started as a personal problem has resulted in a business that has disrupted the online accommodations industry.

Today, the Founders' combined wealth is $12.2 bn. In 2016, Brian Chesky, Joe Gebbia, and Nathan Blecharczyk joined The Giving Pledge, a movement of philanthropists dedicated to giving away the majority of their wealth to charitable causes.

Quotes from the Founders

If we tried to think of a good idea, we wouldn't have been able to think of a good idea. You just have to find the solution for a problem in your own life.

—Brian Chesky

We believe the best solutions come from solving your own problem. If you have a real problem, there's likely someone else who can relate. That's how Airbnb was born.

—Joe Gebbia

SARA BLAKELY, SPANX
A white trouser problem led to a billion dollar empire

Wishing to wear white trousers to a party, Sara realized she didn't have the right underwear to complete the look, so she improvised and cut off the feet to create a footless pantyhose. Knowing that other women may have the same challenge, Sara decided to take her 'crazy idea' forward and use this gap in the market. In 2000, Sara launched Spanx with her $5000 of savings. Within two years, she had completed prototyping, production and gained her first sale at Neiman Marcus, a U.S. retailer.

During the early years, Sara adopted a secondary strategy: The Power of Positioning. Being inspired by brands Kodak and Coca Cola to have the memorable "K" sound in the company name, Sara named the company SPANX. Combining this with a bold positioning strategy; stand out red packaging among a sea of white, black and beige retail products and with accolades from the "Queen of Media", Oprah Winfrey who shared her SPANX experience during her "Favourite Things" segment on television in 2000, catapulted SPANX into the mainstream.

Where are They Today?

20 years on, Spanx is a global company in 50 countries with hundreds of products, employing over 150 people. Before Spanx, "Shapewear" was not even a market segment. Sara's creativity had formed a whole new market consumers didn't know they needed!

Sara turned her $5000 savings into a billion dollar empire and became the youngest self-made female billionaire. In 2012, Blakely was named in *Time* magazine's "Time 100" annual list of the 100 most influential people in the world. Outside of her own business, she co-owns a basketball team, the Atlanta Hawks, and has set up The Spanx by Sara Blakely Foundation to offer scholarships and empower women through education. Sara has also joined The Giving Pledge.

Quotes by Sara Blakely

"There is a hidden blessing in the most traumatic things we go through in our lives. My brain always goes to, 'Where is the hidden blessing? What is my gift?'"

"My Dad encouraged us to fail growing up, he would ask what we failed at that week. If we didn't have something he would be disappointed. It changed my mindset at an early age that failure is not the outcome, failure is not trying. Don't be afraid to fail."

STEVE CHEN and CHAD HURLEY, YOUTUBE
More content is uploaded in 60 days than
3 major networks created in 60 years

Chad Hurley and Steve Chen were inspired to start YouTube after experiencing difficulty sharing a video that Chad took at a dinner party in San Francisco. This frustration led them to question if a faster and better solution could be built. At that time, Vimeo, a video sharing service, was the leading video sharing platform.

In 2005, when Chad and Steve shared their problem story to a group of investors, they jumped on board. A new video sharing service that prioritized video creators was born. By December that year, YouTube had 8 million views per day. By July 2006, 65,000 new videos were being uploaded daily achieving 100 million views. Fast forward 9 years to 2015 and YouTube had 15 billion visitors per month.

Where are They Today?

This exponential growth continued. By February 2017, there were more than 400 hours of content uploaded to YouTube each minute, and one billion hours of content being watched on YouTube every day. As of May 2019, more than 500 hours of video content are uploaded to YouTube every minute. Based on the reported quarterly advertising revenue, YouTube is estimated to have U.S. $15 billion in annual revenues. Google acquired YouTube in 2006 for $1.65 billion. In 2019, YouTube has two billion users worldwide (Statista, 2019). The only social network that has more monthly active users than YouTube is Facebook and generated U.S. $15 billion in ad revenue.

Quotes by Chad Hurley

"If something excites you, go for it!"

"I think success around any product is really about subtle insights. You need a great product and a bigger vision to execute against, but it's really those small things that make the big difference."

NICK WOODMAN, GOPRO
The invention of a passionate surfer leads to sales of 35 million cameras

As a passionate surfer, Nick wanted to film his action on the water in order to demonstrate his skills and fulfill his desire of "going pro." Initially, filming with a camera attached to his hand with rubber bands, he was inspired to create a belt to attach the camera to his body. He used his mother's sewing machine to create the first prototypes and raised money by selling seashells out of his mobile van. In 2002, the idea for GoPro was born. His passion to find a solution that could successfully film on the water took GoPro from a niche product for surfers into the mainstream enabling anyone keen to capture their activities on film. GoPro's fast growth, from selling out of a mobile van to becoming a billion dollar company has made Nick a billionaire.

Where are They Today?

With so much content being created by GoPro users, the company started its transformation to become a media company in 2014 broadcasting its content to YouTube, Virgin America, XBox Live, and the PlayStation network. In 2019, GoPro celebrated selling its 35 millionth HERO camera since the launch of the first HD HERO in 2009.

Nick Woodman's surfing passion led to the creation of the world's most versatile camera that empowers people to be creative, capture their adventures, and share it globally.

Through the Jill and Nicholas Woodman Foundation, donations have been made to a variety of causes, from child abuse prevention to entrepreneur and community building projects.

Quote by Nick Woodman

"As soon as I stopped trying to think about the business idea and started focusing on what I'm passionate about, that's when it came to me."

The POWER OF PROBLEM Exercises

"I'm driven to create something new to solve the problem."

Do you feel this is your Entrepreneur persona? If so, why? If not, why not? Either answer helps provide insights.

Another problem solving example is Ben and Jerry's. School friends Ben Cohen and Jerry Greenfield attended a $5 correspondence ice cream making course in the 1970s. As a result of Ben's inability to taste or smell, chunks of chocolate, fruit, and nuts were added to provide texture to the ice cream and sold in pint tubs. This simple innovation to satisfy the Founder's taste deficit led to a successful global franchise.

1. Do you look at problems from different perspectives and tend to generate multiple solutions?
2. Which problem solving approach are you most drawn to? Algorithms, heuristics, or insights?
3. Do you get inspired thoughts during dream time? If so, how do you capture the ideas?
4. Can you list any three times in your life you have encountered a problem?
5. Did you try an existing product or service to help you overcome it?
6. Could you create something better? If so, what would it do?

Join us

Can you think of other entrepreneurs with this superpower? If you want to meet like minded people or be a contributor sharing real world entrepreneur success stories, please visit www.8superpowers.co.

JOIN the conversation on social media #8superpowers

CHAPTER 2

Power of Perseverance

Perseverance is the ability to keep doing something in spite of the obstacles. People who persevere show steadfastness in doing something despite how hard or how long it takes. A superpower that combines self-belief, tenacity, and determination above and beyond the average person coupled with an immunity to the fear of failure. This mindset can be defined as resilience, grit, and hard work over a period of time despite recurring failures.

Most successful sports people have this superpower. They are not creating a new product, they are the product. Athletes train endlessly to reach the top of their field. Think of the Williams sisters' rise to dominate the world of tennis. It did not happen overnight, it took thousands of hours of practice since the age of four. Olympians train for four years to succeed at one prestigious event. Top performing athletes of all disciplines demonstrate this tenacious, unwavering belief that the product, themselves, can be successful.

Can you develop perseverance? Of course! Carol Dweck, Ph.D., a psychology professor at Stanford University, has spent her career studying motivation and achievement. In her book Mindset: The New Psychology of Success, she presents the difference between a fixed mindset and a growth mindset. A fixed mindset believes their most basic abilities can be developed through dedication and hard work and view their limitations as permanent. A growth mindset interprets challenges and failures as opportunities for personal growth with no boundaries or limitations. Virtually all successful entrepreneurs have a growth mindset.

	Fixed Mindset	**Growth Mindset**
EFFORT	May recruit others to do hard tasks, spending as little effort as possible	Believes good outcomes require effort. It is part of the process
CHALLENGE	Shies away from challenges from fear of failure. Avoids responsibilities.	Challenges are exciting and engaging. They stick to it, mastering the challenge.
MISTAKES and FEEDBACK	Hates making mistakes. Blame others. Defensive when criticized.	Sees the mistake as a lesson to learn from. Doesn't take criticism personally. Open to feedback.

"Perseverance is stubbornness with a purpose."

—Josh Shipp

"Success comes from curiosity, concentration, perseverance and self-criticism."

—Albert Einstein, physicist and developer
of the theory of relativity.

"Many of life's failures are people who did not realize how close they were to success when they gave up."

—Thomas Edison, inventor of the lightbulb.

The Mantra
"I will keep trying until I succeed."

JAMES DYSON, DYSON
5,127 prototypes over 5 years' results in billion dollar empire

James Dyson, the British inventor of the bagless vacuum cleaner famously created 5,127 prototypes over five years before getting it right. Frustration with a clogged vacuum cleaner dust bag reducing suction power, inspired James to design a better solution. James's idea was repeatedly rejected in the UK as his solution would disrupt a $125 million established market for replacement vacuum bags. James' breakthrough moment came when he sought more innovative forward thinking countries. After the product launched on a Japanese shopping channel, it won a design award catapulting sales.

It was ten years before the UK market adopted his Dyson Dual Cyclone cleaner and before long he became the market leader with other leading brands soon developing their cyclonic bagless version.

Thanks to the patented technology, Dyson was able to sue any company that incorporated his unique design. Hoover was the first major company to infringe the design resulting in $5 million of damages.

Where are They Today?

Sir James Dyson, knighted by the Queen, has not only been recognized for his engineering ingenuity but also his contribution to help others. His company invests heavily in research and development, employs over

3500 engineers, participates in numerous university research programs and has set up the Dyson Institute of Engineering and Technology. The James Dyson Foundation inspires young people to be bold, think outside the box, unleash their ideas, and tap into engineering education to bring them to life. A remarkable journey of perseverance led to James Dyson to become one of the world's greatest innovators and engineering champions of our time.

Dyson's superpower has resulted in a personal net worth valued at $13.6 billion and a life of inspiring and giving to future generations of engineers.

Quote by James Dyson

"I made 5,127 prototypes of my vacuum before I got it right. There were 5,126 failures. But I learned from each one. That's how I came up with a solution. So I don't mind failure."

J. K. ROWLING, HARRY POTTER
A 7 year journey of poverty, depression, and rejection led to a $500 million franchise

Having written her first book at the age of 6, Jo's passion for writing continued all through her university days. It was not until 1990, at the age of 25, that Jo conceived the idea for Harry Potter on a delayed train from Manchester to London, mapping out the book series over the next five years. Moving to Portugal to teach English, getting married, and having her first child consumed her time over the coming years. With the marriage breaking down, Jo moved to Edinburgh with her newborn daughter. *"I was jobless, a lone parent, and as poor as it is possible to be in modern Britain without being homeless,"* she said in her commencement speech at Harvard. Suffering from depression, Jo found solace in her writing passion and returned to the idea she conceived on the train. With three chapters complete, she sent the manuscript to many publishers and received twelve rejections. As we know, it only takes one person to embrace an idea for it to become successful and that person was the eight year old daughter of the chairman of Bloomsbury, a publishing house, who was enthralled by the first chapter. This led to a publishing deal and an advance of £1500.

In 1997, when Jo was 32 years old, a 1000 copies of the Philosophers Stone were published. The book won two prestigious children book awards in the following nine months, the Nestle Smarties Book prize and Children's Book of the Year, catapulting the book into the mainstream. Over the next ten years, J. K. Rowling wrote seven Harry Potter books becoming the best-selling book series in history.

Where are They Today?

Since the first book in 1997, 20 years ago, Harry Potter has become one of the most successful global franchises extending across books, films, theme parks, toys, and merchandise grossing $25 billion in revenue.

This is an inspiring "rags to riches" story that has seen Jo become the first billionaire author, winning over twenty awards and being ordained by The Queen with an OBE, Order of the British Empire, for her services to literature and philanthropy. Jo Rowling established the Volant Charitable Trust, to combat poverty and social inequality, and donates to organizations that aid children, one-parent families, and multiple sclerosis research.

Jo Rowling now in her fifties, first conceived the idea for Harry Potter 29 years ago. Her perseverance against all the odds and following her passion has brought joy to millions of people around the world and her legacy will live on for future generations to enjoy.

Quotes by J. K. Rowling

"What was the worst that could happen? Everyone turned me down. Big deal!

"It is impossible to live without failing at something, unless you live so cautiously that you might as well not have lived at all - in which case, you fail by default."

There are many people from all walks of life that epitomize this persona to try, try, and try again.

- Howard Schultz, Founder of Starbucks, was rejected by banks 242 times.
- Actor Sylvester Stallone was rejected 1500 times as the lead character.
- Basketball player, Michael Jordan, who was cut from his high school basketball team said, *"I have been entrusted to take the game winning shot, and I have missed. I have failed over and over and over again in my life. And that is why I succeed."*
- Thomas Edison, one of the greatest inventors of all time, is responsible for inventing the phonograph, the electric light bulb, the movie camera, the microphone, and alkaline batteries. Each invention no doubt required hours of experimentation and failure to bring his inventions to life.

As I write this book during the "Lockdown" as a result of the Coronavirus pandemic sweeping the world, I am in awe of entrepreneurs like Louis Pasteur and Alexander Fleming. They are the pioneers of modern medicine whose discoveries were the first attack on bacteria and viruses. Their breakthroughs have saved millions of lives. Both born in the 18th century, Louis Pasteur, a microbiologist invented the principles of vaccination and pasteurization, and Alexander Fleming discovered penicillin. Imagine how many hours of research, trials, and errors is required to make these discoveries.

Coming back to this century and how our lives have changed within weeks as a result of the invisible, deadly Coronavirus. A new wave of online entrepreneurs are now in the spotlight with innovative products for entertaining, connecting, exercising, and teaching people through the Internet. Imagine if Sir Tim Berners Lee, the inventor of the World Wide Web, heralded as the Top 100 Most Important People of the 20th Century, had not pursued his dream, where would it be right now without the Internet? Which Superpower did Tim Berners Lee have? I'll let you decide.

The Power of Perseverance Exercises
"I will keep trying until I succeed."

Do you feel this is your Entrepreneur persona? If so, why? If not, why not? Either answer helps provide insights.

Whether you are seeking to bring a new idea to market or currently persevering with an existing product, these exercises will help you.

1. Am I willing to still be working on this idea (product/service) in 10 years' time?
2. Do I believe in my idea enough to go through all the trials and tribulations?
3. What problem will my idea be solving? For whom and why?
4. What are the 5 personal sacrifices I will have to make? (Financial, family, social, etc.)
5. Do I have the financial capability to support myself until it succeeds?
6. Who do I need support from during this journey? (Friends, family, mentors, etc.)

Join Us

Can you think of other entrepreneurs with this superpower? If you want to meet like minded people or be a contributor sharing real world entrepreneur success stories, please visit www.8superpowers.co.

JOIN the conversation on social media #8superpowers

CATEGORY 2

Marketing

CHAPTER 3

Power of Positioning

Positioning refers to the place a brand resides in the minds of customers. A positioning strategy is when an entrepreneur identifies a key area to excel in to gain competitive advantage. Key areas include cost, quality, flexibility, speed, and price.

A. **COST positioning** focuses on ways to eliminate costly procedures in order to pass the savings onto the customer. For example, by automating inventory, ordering, and delivery procedures, operational costs are reduced enabling lower prices to be offered.

B. **QUALITY positioning** relies on becoming known for using high quality materials, parts, and suppliers enabling a higher price tag due to excellent materials and performance.

C. **FLEXIBILITY positioning** embraces the ability to change products and services based on customers' changing needs. Many companies find it a challenge to product design, operations, and the team. Introducing new products to meet changing buying needs requires agility, foresight, and vision.

D. **SPEED positioning** allows companies to compete by delivering their product and services quickly to their customers. Glasses R Us champions one hour delivery of eyeglasses.

E. **PRICE positioning** is the approach you take to set the price of the products and services you sell. It requires research, calculations, data, and an understanding of different market factors—like your competitors, consumers ability to pay, market conditions, trade margins, and operating costs. The right pricing strategy gives you the ability to maximize profit. With consumers being savvy on pricing strategies, which entrepreneurs have not only adopted a pricing strategy but also superpowered their way to exponential growth with a disruptive model?

Common pricing strategies are:

Market Focused

1. Penetration pricing is when an introductory low price is offered to entice consumers to buy with the understanding the price will increase in the future.

2. Competition pricing entails offering your product at the same price as your competitors and competing in other ways to gain market share.

3. Bundle pricing models require bundling several products together at a discounted price, thereby creating an enticing single offer.

Consumer Behavior Focused

4. Premium pricing is when a business sets its prices higher than competitors focusing on the prestige, uniqueness, and added value it brings to the consumer.

5. Economy pricing is at the other end of the spectrum to premium pricing widely used by discount retailers targeting price-conscious consumers looking for a "no frills" product or service.

Psychology Focused

6. Price anchoring taps into consumers' cognitive bias. A premium product is placed near a standard product giving the impression the less expensive option is a bargain, making it more likely a consumer will buy that product.

7. Psychology pricing is a strategy that enhances the illusion of value to the customer. The "99 effect" is the most commonly used. Rather than price at $1, price $0.99c, rather than $10, price at $9.99. Studies done by researchers at MIT and the University of Chicago have proven that prices ending in "9" create increased customer demand for the product. The psychological phenomena is driven by the fact that we read left to right, so when we encounter a price of $2.99, we see the 2 first and perceive the price to be closer to $2.00 than it is to $3.00 giving the impression you are offering a great deal.

The Mantra
"I will boldly go where no-one has been before."

SAM WALTON, WALMART
Location scouting by airplane led to $514 billion revenue and the world's largest company

Sam Walton is an example of an effective cost positioning strategy. The Walmart story has been well documented on how "Mr. Sam" constantly adopted innovative strategies over decades to gain and sustain a competitive edge, from his customer centric approach through to discounting prices. The Walmart fifty year story is an inspiring read at www.walmart.com.

For the purposes of this book, let's dive into how Sam Walton boldly went where no one had been before. In 1962, discounting stores popped up all over America, with the three biggest players being Woolworths, K-Mart, and Target. Within five years, K-Mart had 250 stores with sales of $800 million to Walmart's 19 stores and sales of $9 million. Roll on fifty years and KMart has 365 stores with sales of $25 billion to Walmart's 12,000 stores and sales of $500 billion. That is a huge difference. So what strategy did Sam adopt to overcome and ultimately dominate his competitors?

Tapping into his fifteen years' experience at running variety stores in small community towns, Sam Walton saw an opportunity that the larger retailers were not interested in. With the discounting store trend sweeping the United States in the 1960s, the larger retailers believed that a population base of 50,000 was required to be profitable to supply discounted goods. Typically, the larger retailers had warehouses a day's trip away adding additional costs. Sam saw an opportunity. He understood the buying behaviors and customer needs in small towns and sought to capitalize on his knowledge by bringing the discounting trend to towns with smaller populations. His real estate strategy involved buying several stores in suburbs all clustered around the distribution center. In Springfield, Missouri, Walmart had 40 stores within 100 miles. If each store was within an area with a population of 5000, then one distribution center was serving a population of 200,000, at a lower transport cost compared to the larger retailers.

Operating in a pre-digital age without digital maps or efficient transport links between small towns, Sam resourcefully thought outside the box and bought an old plane to scout for locations from the sky. *"The airplane turned into a great tool for scouting real estate. From up in the air, we could check out traffic flows, see which way cities and towns were growing, and evaluate the location of the competition—if there was any. Then we would develop our real estate strategy for that market,"* Sam Walton quote.

This comprehensive understanding of his targeted areas enabled Sam to grow the company exponentially and pass the distribution cost savings onto customers. By the time the competitors realized his strategy, Walmart was opening 50 stores a year compared to their 5.

Sam Walton's positioning superpower embraces the 4 S's approach—Sector, Season, Size, and Saturation.

1. **Sector**

   Operate in a sector where you are experienced. It is obvious but many entrepreneurs try to succeed with a new product in a sector with little knowledge. Sam's customer prowess knowing the buying behaviors in small communities enabled Walmart to meet customer needs.

2. **Season**

   Operate in a sector that is growing or on the leading edge of a trend. In this case, the trend was discounting stores sweeping the United States.

3. **Size**

   What is the size of the sector and who are the leading players? Sam Walton had a thorough understanding of his competitors and sought innovative ways to gain market share.

4. **Saturation**

   As in Sam Walton's case, start small with a few stores, discover your superpower (cost positioning) and saturate the market making it difficult for competitors to enter.

Where are They Today?

Fifty years on, Walmart is a publicly traded family owned business and the world's largest company by revenue, with U.S. $514.05 billion, according to the Fortune Global 500 list in 2019. As of January 2020, Walmart has 11,503 stores and clubs in 27 countries, operating under 56 different names. Sam Walton died in 1992 leaving a legacy of inspiration, innovation, grit, foresight, and determination. The Walmart family is collectively the richest family in the United States and the richest non-royal family in the world. In October 2019, the annual Sunday Times Rich List indicated the Walton family's wealth is at $190.5 billion. The Walmart Foundation regularly donates $1 billion per year to charitable causes.

Quotes by Sam Walton

"There is only one boss - the customer. And he can fire everybody in the company from the chairman on down, simply by spending his money elsewhere."

"Control your expenses better than your competition. This is where you can always find the competitive advantage."

BILL GATES, MICROSOFT
A university dropout revolutionizes the personal computing industry

In 1970, at the age of 15, Bill discovered his passion when a computer was installed at his school. Wanting to know more, his curiosity led to him writing the code for a Tic-tac-toe game in BASIC computing language. Paul Allen, who was equally enthralled by the computer, and Bill became good friends and developed "Traf-o-data," a program that monitored traffic patterns in Seattle. This ability to simplify the complex led to $20,000 revenue and an appetite for business. Bill, a highly intelligent student, followed his parents' desire to attend Harvard University, however, after two years, he dropped out of college to pursue his passion for writing code. In 1975, Bill and Paul formed Microsoft and the first product was BASIC software that ran on an Altair computer. It proved to be a success, and by 1979, Microsoft was grossing $2.5 million; Bill was 23 years old. But, as we all know, this was only the beginning.

This was the era of the third industrial revolution, with the birth of the quaternary (tech) sector, where companies like Apple, Intel, and IBM were developing hardware and riding the wave of success at the forefront of the industry. Bill stayed true to his passion for developing software products and believed that this would bring him more fortune. For him, this was not just about software products, there was a bigger bolder vision, *"How does Microsoft become the intelligence that runs on all computers?"*

There were several game changing moments that define the superpower Bill adopted. Bill had the ability to simplify the complex so he could feature in the Power of Process chapter. He also was an advocate for hiring clever people to help build the company tapping into the Power of People. However, in my opinion, it was the following strategies and decisions that led to Microsoft's exponential growth.

The first defining decision Bill made was rather than give away your code, like most were doing, charge people for it. At the time, among the developer community, this was met with animosity. Bill believed that in order to gain quality software and enable continuous innovation, payment should be made. Microsoft's first client, IBM wished to buy the code, however, Bill proposed they pay a licensing fee for software sold on their computers. Adopting a quality positioning strategy led to an explosion in the company's revenue, from $16 million in 1979 to $25 million in 1981. By 1983, an estimated 30% of the world's computers ran on its software.

Another defining moment in the history of Microsoft was Bill's bold approach and marketing tactics to position Microsoft ahead of its current capability and reality. Some may call this overpromising, others call it bluffing. It is actually an innovation positioning strategy. In 1981, Apple invited Microsoft to develop software for the MacIntosh. At this point Microsoft software operated as a text, keyboard driven MS-DOS system. While working with Apple, Bill was introduced to the graphic interface in development at Apple. Around the same time, Bill announced Microsoft had a graphic interface that would be compatible with all the products on MS-DOS, called Windows. However, no such product was in development at the time. It was actually *two years later* when Microsoft introduced Windows. This bold innovation positioning strategy paid off. 30% of the world's computers were using MS-DOS and were willing to wait for the new Windows product versus changing systems.

With responsibility for product strategy, Bill and by default, Microsoft, was often under investigation for its marketing tactics and monopoly on operating systems for PC's. It is Bill's deep belief in software and the positioning strategies that led to the company's exponential growth. Competitors at the time were one product companies, Microsoft was an innovative multi-product company scything through the industry.

When Microsoft went public, Bill was 31 years old owning 45% shares, valuing his net worth at $234 million. Between 2009 to 2014, Bill's wealth doubled from $40 billion to $82 billion.

Where are They Today?

In 2014, age 59, Bill Gates stepped down as chairman of Microsoft. He is considered as one of the top 100 people who influenced the 20th century and revolutionized the personal computing industry. A fanatical teenager, passionate about coding software, grew up to be one of the world's most inspirational people.

With a continual passion to solve problems, Bill co-founded the Bill and Melinda Gates Foundation, with his wife with the belief that "all lives have equal values." One of the largest private foundations in the world, it has donated $50.1 billion since inception and employs 1,489 people passionate about improving health and alleviating poverty globally.

Quote by Bill Gates

"I am a great believer that any tool that enhances communication has profound effects in terms of how people can learn from each other, and how they can achieve the kind of freedoms that they're interested in."

STEVE JOBS, APPLE ITUNES MUSIC STORE
How a $0.99c irresistible offer changed the entire music industry

Steve Jobs, a visionary who brought us Apple's revolutionary products, the iPod, iPhone, and iPad and his career journey has been widely documented globally. Consumers are happy with Apple's premium pricing for the innovative products, however, for the purpose of this book, I would like to champion the genius pricing model Steve Jobs introduced, which disrupted the music industry.

Apple is a technology company in the business of connecting people's passion for music and photos through cool devices. Back in the 2000s, the music industry was on the backfoot trying to overcome piracy and protect artists' copyright as file sharing services, like Napster, were on the rise. Steve approached five record labels with a plan to provide an online music store enabling customers to purchase, play, download, and organize their music in one place and offer all music for $0.99c, a one size fits all pricing model. This pricing model was disruptive. How could you offer a number 1 best-selling song for the same price as a throw away B side song? With record labels and artists seeking a legitimate solution to combat the rise in piracy, they agreed to the partnership.

The iTunes Store launched in 2003 with 200,000 songs. In the first week, 1 million songs were downloaded and by the end of the first year, Apple celebrated 100 million songs sold. Steve had created the first legal digital music store with an irresistible pricing model at its heart.

Where are They Today?

The Apple Music Store evolved into a multimedia store, offering 60 million songs, 2.2 million Apps, 25,000 TV shows and 65,000 films. In 2019, Apple announced the iTunes Store would cease to exist in its current form and adapt again to meet the change in consumer behaviors where content is available on Apple Music, Apple TV, and Apple Podcasts.

Steve Jobs passed away at the age of 56 years after battling with pancreatic cancer. A global icon whose legacy lives on in this fourth industrial revolution. Steve's wife, Laurene Powell Jobs, inherited the wealth and plans to give away her billions during her lifetime through the social change organization, Emerson Collective, she founded.

Quotes by Steve Jobs

"Because the people who are crazy enough to think they can change the world are the ones who do."

"Being the richest man in the cemetery doesn't matter to me. Going to bed at night saying we've done something wonderful, that's what matters to me."

"Let's go invent tomorrow rather than worrying about yesterday."

The Power of Positioning Exercises

"I will boldly go where no-one has been before."

Do you feel this is your Entrepreneur persona? If so, why? If not, why not? Either answer helps provide insights.

THE 4 S's

SECTOR

1. Do you have experience in the sector you are in or seek to operate in?
2. How many years' experience?
3. What level of expertise/qualifications can you tap into to elevate your positioning?
4. What other experts can you bring on board to help you?

SEASON

5. Is the sector growing?
6. Have you completed market research into the sector trends? Year on year growth rates?

SIZE

7. What is the size of the opportunity?
8. Why is your product/service ideally positioned to attract customers and generate revenue?

SATURATION

9. Have you completed market research into the competitive landscape? How many competitors? Market share?
10. What do you offer that your competitors don't?

PRICING

11. Which pricing strategy does your current product/service adopt?
12. List 3 reasons why you chose that strategy.
13. Have you experimented with any other pricing strategies?
14. List 3 ways you could implement a pricing model that would appeal to the masses.
15. List another example of each pricing model below:
    a. Penetration pricing (Netflix)
    b. Competition pricing (Shopify)
    c. Bundle pricing (Walmart)
    d. Premium pricing (Rolex)
    e. Economy pricing (Dollar stores)
    f. Psychology pricing (Amazon)
16. Many other pricing models exist. Name 3 others that you have come across in everyday life.

Join Us

Can you think of other entrepreneurs with this superpower? If you want to meet like minded people or be a contributor sharing real world entrepreneur success stories, please visit www.8superpowers.co.

JOIN the conversation on social media #8superpowers

CHAPTER 4

Power of Proximity

Proximity

/prɒkˈsɪmɪti/

Nearness in space, time, or relationship

Imagine if you can be successful simply by being in close proximity to the right people in the right place. Would you move to a new city to immerse yourself into an ecosystem to maximize your success?

> *Proximity is power. If you can get proximity with people that are the best in the world, things can happen because of all of the people they know, the insights they have and the life experience they have. They can save you a decade of time by one insight.*
>
> —Tony Robbins

> *The Proximity Principle: To do what I want to do I have to be around the people who are doing it and the places it is happening.*
>
> —Ken Coleman

Originally proposed by social psychologist Leon Festinger in the 1950s, the proximity or propinquity effect is the idea that physical and/or psychological closeness increases familiarity and attraction. Increased interaction is also a factor, as people tend to form friendships with those they encounter more often. According to psychologist Theodore Newcomb, proximity promotes readiness of communication, as a result of which, individuals have an opportunity to discover each other's common attitudes.

The two popular principles are:

1. **People Proximity**
   We become who we hang out with.
   > —Napoleon Hill, best-selling author
   > of Think and Grow Rich.

   You are the average of the five people you spend most time with.
   > —Jim Rohn.

Research by Harvard social psychologist Dr. David McClelland demonstrated that the people you habitually associate with determine as much as 95% of your success or failure in life.

In the realm of dating, apps like Tinder have been built on the premise that a matching algorithm will identify people who have similar attitudes, values, hobbies, and desires within close geographical proximity. Tinder pioneered the use of location technology to identify matches in real time and coupled it with the "swipe right" if you like a person, thereby gamifying the dating experience. With an annual growth rate of 11.6%, the online dating segment is projected to reach U.S. $2.725 million in 2020 as people continue to seek their ideal partner by tapping into the power of proximity.

2. **Place Proximity**

Place proximity can be seen in effect at both macro and micro levels.

Macro Level

A business cluster is a geographic concentration of interconnected businesses, suppliers, and talent in a particular field. The benefits of enhanced innovation and productivity far outweigh the downside of competitive closeness. Many examples across industries exist where clusters of commerce have been created to enable enhanced innovation and productivity between like-minded people.

- Covering 120 km, Silicon Valley is one of the densest ecosystems comprising over 2000 companies.
- The WISTA Science and Technology Park in Berlin is home to 800 companies, making it Germany's largest science park.
- Motorsport Valley in the UK is a center of manufacturing excellence comprising 4,300 companies, employing 41,000 people and home to eight out of the ten Formula One teams.
- Spreading over 600 km, Genome Valley in Hyderabad, India is a cluster for 150 life science companies.

People choose to work in these ecosystems to tap into the Power of Proximity.

There are numerous stories of people being discovered and new products created, by simply being in the right place at the right time. At 18 years old, aspiring model Charlize Theron moved from South Africa to the world's largest hub of entertainment companies, Hollywood, only to be discovered while in a queue at a bank. Now Charlize is a multi-award winning actress and a Time 100 most influential people in the world.

Would energy drink Red Bull exist if Dietrich Mateschitz had not visited Thailand thirty years ago? Dietrich Mateschitz traveled to Thailand where he met Chaleo Yoovidhya who gave him a drink, Krating Daeng, to help cure his jet lag. Impressed with the effects, Mateschitz partnered with Yoovidhya to introduce the re-branded drink, Red Bull, to the international market. Since launch, Red Bull has sold 75 billion cans in 171 countries, becoming the market leader in energy drinks.

Micro Level

Supermarkets are masters of utilizing the proximity effect to make you buy specific goods. From placing unknown brands adjacent to well-known brands, to positioning products at the checkout for ease of purchase.

As smart cities grow and IoT (Internet of Things) becomes part of our everyday lives, more companies are tapping into this technological power to tailor a customer's experience based on their immediate location. Proximity marketing is a hyper localized strategy that provides a customer experience tailored to a location. Great examples include:

- Retail giant Nike has 40 beacons in the Shanghai store to detect the shoes customers are trying on and subsequently display the relevant information on surrounding digital screens. A full customer experience enables reservation, collection, and payment to be made alleviating the need to queue at checkouts.
- The Starbucks mobile app allows customers to place orders, pay in store, collect rewards.
- EAT, the food-to-go chain, overhauled its in-store and online experience declaring proximity marketing as a core "strategic pillar" to enable the company to access more information about customer behavior and drive business intelligence to make precise decisions about how consumer behavior can be influenced.
- Walmart embedded beacons into light bulbs throughout the store to track shoppers' behavior and send push notifications about discount coupons to in-store customers.

These are hyper localized campaigns designed to enhance the in-store customer experience and generate higher revenue.

The power of proximity also extends to the workplace. Research from the Kellogg School of Management at Northwestern University discovered high performers raised the performance of those who sat within a 25-foot radius by an average of 15%, estimating an additional $1 million in annual profits.

The Mantra
"Right people, right place."

"Right time, right place, right people equals success. Wrong time, wrong place, wrong people, equals most of the real human history."

Idries Shah

TINDER
Proximity technology leads to 8 billion love matches

In 2012, six people, Sean Rad, Jonathan Badeen, Justin Mateen, Joe Munoz, Dinesh Moorjaniu, and Whitney Wolfe, founded the dating app Tinder. For the purposes of our story, we will follow the entrepreneurial path of just one, Sean Rad.

Originally seeking to be a performer, Sean Rad changed career direction after a high school internship exposed the inner workings of the entertainment sector. He reverted to his passion for technology, which he discovered at 13 years old, after being gifted a mobile phone by his parents. Sean's first tech startup was Orgoo, an ecommerce platform, while at college. His next venture was a social media branding app, Adly.

Sean dropped out of college and joined a mobile app incubator, Hatch Labs to work on Cardify, a credit card loyalty app. It was during a hackathon that the idea for a hot-or-not dating app, Matchbox, was hatched. The idea tapped into the proximity principle that you feel more comfortable to approach somebody if you know they are like minded and live locally.

Matchbox won the hackathon. After three weeks' development time and a $50,000 investment, Matchbox relaunched as Tinder introducing college students to the app via influencer marketing. In less than 2 months, 1 million matches had been made.

In an increasingly competitive market, with match.com leading the way, it was the introduction, in 2012, of the "swipe right" functionality that resulted in Tinder being named "the dating industry disruptor." Seeking a way to organize photos within the App, co-founder Jonathan Badeen was inspired with a method after getting out of a shower swiping the mirror to see his face. On Tinder, swiping right indicates that one is attracted to the person and if they similarly swipe right on your photo, a match is made. By 2014, users were swiping 1 billion times a day.

Since launch, Tinder has been downloaded 340 million times, has 57 million active users, of which 6 million are paying subscribers generating $1.2 billion in revenue. Tapping into the power of proximity has made Tinder one of the highest grossing non-gaming apps to date.

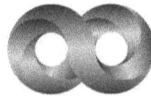

The Billionaire Making Places of the World

At the beginning of the century, a *billionaire* individual did not exist. Today, there are over 2,825 billionaires and counting. Are there certain cities and regions that harvest more billionaires than others? Is the power of place proximity the reason for these clusters of billionaires?

Table 4.1 2019 Billionaire population and total wealth by region

Region	Total number of billionaires	Increase on previous year	Wealth ($bn)	Increase on previous year
Europe	847	6.9%	$2,449 bn	8.2%
North America	834	11.2%	$3,527 bn	13.8%
Asia	758	12%	$2,402	11%
Middle East	172	–1.1%	$450 bn	1.6%
Latin America & The Caribbean	140	–1.4%	$450 bn	2.4%
Africa	41	5.1%	$88 bn	6.2%
Pacific	33	10%	$69 bn	6.7%
Total	2,825	8.5%	$9,435	10.3%

Source: Wealth-X

Europe remains the region with the largest number of billionaires, with Asia recording the fastest rise, and North America recording the most dynamic gain in wealth. An 8.5% annual rise in the number of billionaires globally with an increased wealth of 10.3%.

Table 4.2 2019 Billionaire population and total wealth by country

Rank	Country	Number of Billionaires	Wealth ($bn)
1	United States	788	3,431
2	China	342	1,151
3	Germany	153	477
4	Russia	114	390
5	Switzerland	100	274
6	United Kingdom	100	217
7	Hong Kong	96	280
8	India	87	314
9	Saudi Arabia	62	152
10	France	60	219
11	Italy	53	157
12	Brazil	50	162
13	United Arab Emirates	47	163
14	Canada	46	96
15	Singapore	45	87

Source: Wealth-X

Table 4.3 2019 Billionaire population and total wealth by city

Rank	City	Number of Billionaires
1	New York	113
2	Hong Kong	96
3	San Francisco	77
4	Moscow	73
5	London	66
6	Beijing	57
7	Singapore	45
8	Los Angeles	44

Rank	City	Number of Billionaires
9	Shenzhen	39
10	Mumbai	38
11	Dubai	35
12	São Paulo	33
13	Istanbul	32
14	Hangzhou	32
15	Tokyo	30

Source: Wealth-X

The top 15 cities are home to 29% of the global billionaire population, with New York being the largest billionaire population of any city globally.

58% of billionaires are self-made, 88% are male, and 12% female. 10% of billionaires are under 50 years old, with the majority, 50%, in the 50 to 70 years age group, and the remaining 40% in the over 70 category.

Philanthropy is the favorite passion followed by sports, aviation, and politics. Showcasing the zero to hero stories and the superpower strategies adopted by billionaires inspires and educates us all, however, for me, discovering how billionaires distribute their wealth to help humanity and the planet, remains at the heart of this book.

Societal expectations of "giving back" have risen, regardless of whether you are rich or poor. From small acts of kindness and charity runs to championing front line workers during Covid, the human consciousness has been raised. Chapter 8 shines the spotlight on entrepreneurs who have tapped into the Power of the Planet.

Among the billionaire population, the leading philanthropic cause is education, with almost eight in every 10 billionaires directing part of their philanthropy to this field. Social services, healthcare and medical research, and the Arts follow. Between January and May 2020, 10% of billionaires diverted their philanthropic focus towards Covid-19 causes to help find a cure to save humanity. Of these billionaires, 89% were male and 85% were over 50 years old.

The Power of Proximity Exercises

"Right people, right place."

Do you feel this is your Entrepreneur persona? If so, why? If not, why not? Either answer helps provide insights.

1. List 5 ways you can tap into the power of proximity in your current scenario.
2. People—Who do you need to be in close proximity to? And why?
3. Place—Where do you need to be? Either physically or virtually? And why?
4. How long will it take to implement your plan?
5. What additional goals will you achieve in the next 1 to 3 years if you adopt proximity strategies?
6. What are the consequences if you do not implement the strategies?

Join Us

Can you think of other entrepreneurs with this superpower? If you want to meet like minded people or be a contributor sharing real world entrepreneur success stories, please visit www.8superpowers.co.

JOIN the conversation on social media #8superpowers

CATEGORY 3

Masses

CHAPTER 5

Power of People

This chapter focuses on entrepreneurs who have harnessed the Power of People as their primary superpower to succeed eons above and beyond the norm. There are three approaches—Mirror Mentors, Beef Up the Board, and Community Builders.

1. **Mirror Mentors**

Mentors offer personal support and advice to entrepreneurs, not the broader company. Advisors work on behalf of the company and its shareholders. By having a mentor who has "been there, seen it, and done it!" acting as a sounding board enables the entrepreneur to share the peaks and troughs of building a business with a trusted person. Mentors can exist in many forms; a mentor can be a role model who an entrepreneur may want to emulate, or they may be someone who has created a step by step guide and laid out the path to success in a book and course, or someone who regularly speaks to the entrepreneur. Most successful entrepreneurs can tell you who was their first mentor and how they helped to inspire them to follow their path and maximize their capabilities.

The Mantra
"I want to be like you, teach me"

TONY ROBBINS
Pay it forward: A 17 year old meets a mentor that sets him on a path to coach 50 million people globally

Having an unhappy childhood and a lack of a role model within his family, Tony found solace in reading books on human development and biographies of successful people. The realization that many of the greatest people on the planet have endured the greatest challenges and turned their suffering into service inspired Tony to expand his quest from devouring books to attending seminars to meet mentors face to face.

Tony had three key mentors that entered his life at various stages. At 17 years old, Tony met his first mentor, Jim Rohn, a motivational speaker, author, and a self-made millionaire. Inspired at a young age, Tony Robbins now looks back on this and says on his website that he learnt the Power of Change from Jim. "He taught me that if you want anything to change, *you* must change. If you want things to get better, *you've* got to get better."

Now in his 20's, Tony encountered his next inspirational mentor, John Grinder, the father of Neuro-linguistic Physiology (NLP) who taught him the Power of Physiology and the principle that "success leaves clues." Imagine finding someone whose results you want, studying them, then mirroring them to become a master yourself.

Tony's third mentor, Peter Gruber taught him the Power of Storytelling. How to discover your authentic self, be compassionate, and unleash a story that will inspire others. Tony has put this advice to great use and is now known for his immersive global live events of helping others along a journey of self-discovery and mastery.

Where are They Today?

Over the last four decades, Tony Robbins has dedicated his life to paying forward the knowledge he accrued from his mentors. His website states, "Tony Robbins is an entrepreneur, bestselling author, philanthropist and the nation's #1 Life and Business Strategist. Author of five internationally bestselling books, including the recent New York Times #1 best-seller UNSHAKEABLE, Mr. Robbins has empowered more than 50 million people from 100 countries through his audio, video and life training programs. He created the #1 personal and professional development program of all time, and more than 4 million people have attended his live seminars."

Tapping into his own personal experience, Tony is passionate that no person has to suffer. Over 10 years ago, Tony partnered with Feeding America with the initial challenge of providing 100 million meals. Harnessing the power of a tribe, with a following of more than 20 million on social media, Tony regularly raises awareness across his platforms and has successfully attracted a further 5000 new partners to Feeding America. The new ambition is to donate 1 billion meals by 2025.

Quotes by Tony Robbins

"If you want to be successful find someone who has achieved the results you want and copy what they do and you'll achieve the same results"

"You become who you spend time with."

WARREN BUFFET
**An investment book unlocked a passion
resulting in the world's richest man**

Warren made his first investment at 11 years old after being introduced to stockbroking by his father. He continued to show entrepreneurial prowess with his passion to make money, and during his teenage years, Warren pursued a range of ventures, from selling a horse racing tip sheet to installing a pinball machine at a barbershop. Keen to learn about business at just 16 years old, he attended University to study the subject.

It was a book, The Intelligent Investor by Benjamin Graham, that sparked his passion for investing. So much so, Warren chose to study under Benjamin Graham by attending Columbia Business School. After gaining his master's degree, he worked for his mentor at Graham-Newman Corp before setting up his own company, Buffet Partnership. The skills he learnt from his mentor in identifying undervalued companies led to Warren becoming a millionaire by 31 years old.

Where are They Today?

As of December 2019, Warren Buffet's net worth was U.S. $88.9 billion making him the fourth wealthiest person in the world. Deemed to be the most successful investor in the world, it is his inspirational philanthropic approach that sets him apart. Yearning to contribute back to the world, he set up the Giving Pledge with his long term friend, Bill Gates in 2010, where billionaires pledge to give away their wealth to help solve world problems. As of May 2019, The Giving Pledge had 209 members, ranging from 30 to 90 years old, from 22 countries, with contributions of over $500 billion.

Quotes by Warren Buffet

"It's better to hang out with people better than you. Pick out associates whose behaviour is better than yours and you'll drift in that direction."

"The best investment you can make, is an investment in yourself. The more you learn, the more you'll earn."

2. **Beef up the Board**

We have looked at the Power of People on a one to one basis, let's now look at the power of gaining 5 to 10 non-employee people.

A confident entrepreneur with heightened self-awareness seeks to hire more experienced people than themselves to gain credibility and accelerate company growth faster. This strategy satisfies investors and customers as the company appears highly professional, capable, and robust. Engagement of their services may be immersive or infrequent depending on what the startup can afford at that time or the company's growth phase, from seed to Series B.

This approach is now widely used in the startup ecosystem resulting in a new trend for companies to hire in Advisory Panels. But crucially, they are not mentors to the executive team or employees of the company, they only advise. The typical advisory topics range from business expertise in strategy and business development to sector specific expertise in media, legal, medical, for example. Often a seasoned Advisor brings their wealth of experience of 5 to 10 startups at a time, thereby creating a "Portfolio Career." It is a win-win for both the entrepreneur and the advisor.

3. **Community builders**

"I will create a tribe to succeed"

Building a loyal tribe of brand evangelists is a powerful yet under-utilized success strategy. Attracting like-minded people passionate about your cause, building trust, and empowering them with the tools to broadcast the brand message to their followers requires vision, planning, and time. To build a community, you have to stand for something, be a champion that moves people to follow your vision.

5 key steps to building a community:

1. **Strategy**
   o What is the vision and purpose of the community? Write it down.
   o What problem are they helping you solve? What mission do you champion?
   o Why would they become brand evangelists? What is in it for them?
   o What is the tribe mission statement?

2. **Leadership**
   o Find a leader who the community would respect.
   o Write a summary biography highlighting their passion, credentials and why this person is the community leader.
   o Identify 2 to 4 next level brand ambassadors to help attract and onboard the community.

3. **Culture**
   o Create a "Culture Deck." It is a summary of the core values and beliefs of a company. With startup, success relies on hiring the right people and attracting the right partners and clients. A culture deck cements in their mind you know your direction of travel.
   o Success leaves clues. Read the other culture decks such as Zappos and Netflix which have paved the way for many companies.
   o Use the 8P Culture Deck Template. I have created Culture Decks for several startups following the 8P format. If you would like to download a copy, please visit www.superpower.co free tools and resources tab.

4. **Community management**

- o As the community, tribe, and followers grow, a management team is required to plan, implement, and deliver the tools, from software, applications, templates to guides, they need to champion the brand.
- o Allocate a community management budget. Appoint the management team.
- o Name the community. There are several types of communities from sales people— Introducers and Affiliates, to celebrities endorsing the brand— Ambassadors—to social media Influencers. Each type requires a different approach and engagement plan.
- o Create an introductory pack for each type outlining the vision, mission, culture, and goals.
- o Create an engagement plan with online and offline initiatives.
- o Agree metrics for executives and operational management.

5. **Feedback**

- o Listen to the comments and feedback from the tribe.
- o With a distributed community, set up an online forum for discussion, such as a monthly meetup, to share ideas and best practices.
- o Stay agile. Pivot quickly. Respond to their needs.
- o The goal is to become a highly networked group of individuals passionate about a common cause.

NICK SWINMURN and TONY HSIEH, ZAPPOS
A happy tribe built a $1.2 billion company

In 1999, while shopping for shoes, Nick became frustrated when the high street retailers he visited did not have the right size and color of the Airwalk Chukka Boots he required. Confident he was not the only customer having this problem, Nick quit his day job to set up an online shoe retailer ShoeSite.com and left a voicemail for Tony Hsieh at Venture Frogs. Tony in his book "Delivering Happiness : A path to Profits, Passion and Purpose" heralds Nick's factual voicemail as the hook that led Venture

Frogs to invest $2 million. The factoid was that 5% of the $40 billion shoe business was already being done through mail order. "*That was my big statistic. People were already buying shoes without trying them o*n." Nick shared in an interview with Footwear News.

Over the coming five years, the company experienced exponential growth under the new company name, Zappos, with Tony as co-CEO. Year 1 saw $1.6 million in gross sales, Year 2 $8.6 million rising to $184 million by 2004. This five year growth attracted a $35 million investment to enable further scaling, and by 2008, within nine years, Zappos celebrated U.S.D $1 billion in annual sales. In 2009, Amazon acquired Zappos for $1.2 billion.

So, what Superpower did the Zappos Founders adopt to go from zero to hero in less than ten years?

The power of a tribe. Hiring the right people passionate about a collaborative way of working where everyone's idea and opinion mattered, layered with the hypothesis that if the company was good to the employees, this would translate through to a happy customer experience. Better service, repeat customers, low marketing costs, long term profits, and fast growth. The catch phrase "*Delivering Wow*" was at the heart of the Zappos culture.

From an early stage, Tony took a tribe led approach, from crowdfunding the company's "10 Values" from Zappos people through to enabling everyone to be active on their social media accounts sharing their life at Zappos. Tony quotes, "*There's three types of happiness and really happiness is about being able to combine pleasure, passion, and purpose in one's personal life. I think it's helpful and useful to actually think about all three in terms of how you can make customers happier, employees happier, and ultimately, investors happier.*" By hiring a tribe of passionate people keen to live and work in a happiness culture led to exponential growth.

Where are They Today?

Nick left Zappos in 2006 and has set up a number of companies since. Tony is the billionaire CEO who famously lives in an Airstream caravan on the Zappos site, called the Downtown Project in

Las Vegas, another Zappos social experiment that became successful among employees. His book "Delivering Happiness" is a New York Times bestseller and is seen as a handbook for many corporations on how to build successful community tribes. After 21 years, in August 2020, Tony announced his retirement as CEO of Zappos and plans to support philanthropic causes and entrepreneurs who are working for social good.

Quotes from the Founders

Our customers and the word of mouth they've spread about Zappos have been the greatest reason for our success. We realise that and are focused continually doing whatever we can to improve their experience.

—Nick Swinmurn

Business often forget about the culture, and ultimately, they suffer for it because you can't deliver good service from unhappy employees.

—Tony Hsieh

JAY SHETTY
A monk builds a tribe of 35 million followers within 4 years

Jay's difficult childhood features insecurity, bullying, the sudden death of two teenage friends, and being suspended multiple times from school. It was at 18 years old, Jay met a monk who inspired him greatly with his outlook, authenticity, and passion to serve. At 22, after graduating, Jay adopted the monk's lifestyle in India and Europe, studying timeless philosophies, learning mindfulness techniques, and helping communities through food programs.

After 3 years, Jay returned to his parents seeking the next chapter in his life. To get back into corporate life, his friends invited him to guest speak at conferences about the lessons he learnt living as a monk. In 2016, realizing the world was becoming digital and his unique perspective was helping people, Jay started making videos. His breakthrough moment came when media mogul Arianna Huffington saw his videos and invited Jay to host the HuffPost Lifestyle segment. This exposure catapulted Jay into the mainstream enabling him to show his authentic passion to serve.

Where are They Today?

Jay set up his own video agency and has become one of the most popular storytellers of our time. His videos have been viewed 4 billion times by his 35 million following, making him one of the most viewed people internationally and being named Forbes "Europe's 30 under 30" list for his role as a game changer and influencer in the world of media.

So how did Jay go from zero to hero in four years? The answer comes down to his clear purpose "TO MAKE WISDOM GO VIRAL." By sharing his monk mindset daily, across multiple platforms, Jay built a tribe passionate to learn his wisdom and pay it forward. With 35 million followers within 4 years, Jay has become one of the world's most inspirational personal development coaches.

Jay's philanthropic focus has been on unleashing the potential in children globally via charities Kailash Satyarthi Children's Foundation and Pencils of Promise. 152 million children are child laborers worldwide. 263 million are out of school. Both charities envision a world where all children are free to be children and get an education.

Quotes by Jay Shetty

When your focus is a success and you don't get you a break, it will break you. When your focus is service, you'll never need a break because there are so many opportunities.

Create meaningful, purposeful, and fulfilling life for yourself and use that to make an impact and difference in the lives of others.

The Power of People Exercises

"I want to be like you, teach me" and
"I will create a tribe to succeed"

Do you feel this is your Entrepreneur persona? If so, why? If not, why not? Either answer helps provide insights.

MENTORS

1. List your Top 5 current mentors (books you read, people you follow on social media, etc.).
2. List 5 core values these mentors have that align with your values.
3. List your top 3 goals for the next 12 months.
4. Can these mentors provide the toolkit (products) to help you succeed? Yes/No.
5. If not, name 3 additional mentors you would like to help you. (Mentors can be family and friends through to online gurus you wish to mirror.)

ADVISORS

6. What skills gaps do you have in the company (from accountant, legal to strategy, and business development)?
7. Research 3 people in each category that are experts in their field.
8. Contact them and invite them to join your team of advisors.

TRIBE

9. List 5 people that would be an ideal Ambassador for your company?
10. Identify 5 social media influencers that could spread the word about your company.
11. Create a "Culture Deck" listing your core values and what the company represents.
12. List 3 ways to empower your team to contribute. Share with your tribe.

Join Us

Can you think of other entrepreneurs with this superpower? If you want to meet like minded people or be a contributor sharing real world entrepreneur success stories, please visit www.8superpowers.co.

JOIN the conversation on social media #8superpowers

CHAPTER 6

Power of Partnerships

There are many reasons companies choose to collaborate, from leveraging each other's expertise to entering a new market or territory.

A partnership

- Fuels innovation
- Decreases costs as a result of pooling resources
- Increases productivity
- Instant gain in people, infrastructure, culture, regulation
- Achieves rapid strategic growth
- Offers access to both local and distant markets
- Economies of scale and market power

Types of Partnerships

Strategic Alliance

Strategic alliances are on the rise. According to PwC, 48% of global CEO's planned to pursue a strategic alliance in 2019. In a continually unstable economic climate, a strategic partnership can help drive corporate growth and help companies win. It is a collaborative agreement between two or more companies that come together for a mutually beneficial goal while remaining separate entities. Some alliances provide organizations with a new set of skills or capabilities, others seek the opportunity to cross sell products into a new customer base. They are an alternative to the organic option of building a new business from the ground up, or the organic option of making an acquisition. The strategic alliance is planned and executed by representatives of both companies.

Successful Strategic Alliances

Music and Transport: Spotify and Uber partnered to provide streaming services to Uber riders. Not every Spotify customer uses Uber, nor does every Uber rider have a Spotify account. By offering this service enabled each company to attract new customers from each other's customer base.

Creativity and Tech: The Hewlett Packard and Disney alliance was born as a result of Disney purchasing audio equipment from Hewlett Packard during the creation of Fantasia. Fast forward to today, this successful alliance sees HP systems embedded at Disney attractions, such as Disney's Mission: SPACE to enable a thrilling technologically advanced ride.

Coffee and Books: A book browsing experience is enhanced by the strategic alliance between Barnes & Noble and Starbucks. Grab a coffee while reviewing the latest bestselling books all in one place.

Airline Alliances: Both One World and Star Alliance are examples of a whole sector alliances. The codeshare agreement enables two or more airlines to publish and market the same flight under their own airline and flight number. This results in cost reductions from shared sales offices, operational facilities, and staff, which is passed onto the traveler through lower prices, greater flight choice, and access to a range of services such as airport lounges and a loyalty reward scheme.

Unsuccessful Strategic Alliances

The majority of alliances fail to achieve their objectives. According to Forbes, the termination rate for alliances is close to 80%. The need for trust, collaboration, and risk sharing makes an alliance a challenging option. Even an obvious pairing can fail.

Jewelry and Watches: On paper, this seemed an obvious collaboration with Tiffany & Co entering a license and distribution agreement with Swatch to manufacture Tiffany & Co brand watches. With delays in product development and a favored marketing position to Swatch customers, Tiffany & Co became a disgruntled partner and failed to market the watch resulting in an unprofitable venture. This 20 year agreement lasted only 3 years resulting in each party suing each other in 2014.

> *We signed a partnership thinking it was going to work perfectly, and it failed dramatically. To be successful today you have to be true to your DNA, and there's no way an external company can take care of that as you do. You don't just give away your brand to someone who might have completely different objectives.*
>
> —Nicola Andreatta,
> VP and General Manager of Tiffany & Co Swiss Watches

Toys and Petrol: In 2011, Lego formed a co-branded partnership with oil company Shell enabling shell-branded toys to be sold in gas stations. This partnership resulted in a public outcry. So where did it go wrong? The companies had misaligned core values. Lego is a children's brand known for its social and environmental values. By partnering with Shell, a company associated with pollution, the Lego brand values were in question. Having built a trusted customer base, it is key that a company examines the relationships they have with other companies ensuring alignment; otherwise, they risk alienating customers. In 2014, Lego did not renew the contract.

Joint Venture

A joint venture is the next level in which two or more businesses sign a contractual agreement thereby creating a third, jointly owned company sharing in the profit and losses. Typically a new management team oversees the joint venture.

Successful Joint Ventures

Life Science and Drugmaker: Alphabet (Google's parent company) and GlaxoSmithKline entered a joint venture under which the two companies planned to invest $715 million over seven years to research treating diseases with electrical signals. According to Bloomberg, GlaxoSmithKline has 55% of the joint venture and Google-parent Alphabet 45%.

Car Manufacturer and Ride Hailing Service: Volvo and Uber entered a 50:50 joint venture to produce self-driving cars with $300 million investment. Uber will purchase Volvos and install a driverless control system for the needs of its ride-hailing service.

Tea, Coffee and India: Tata Global Beverages and Starbucks created Tata Starbucks in 2012, a 50:50 joint venture to penetrate the India market. With Starbucks' established retail brand experience combined with the world's second largest producer of tea, Tata Global Beverages, 167 stores across India have opened to date.

Unsuccessful Joint Ventures

Car manufacturer enters China market: In 1996, Italian car manufacturer Fiat sought to enter the Chinese market through a 50:50 joint venture with Nanjing Auto. The vision was to combine foreign capital, technology, local operations, and government expertise. Over the next six years, only four models were built and sales were low at 25,000 cars annually. What went wrong? Nanjing Auto was the wrong partner. Known primarily for making trucks, the customer did not adopt this new line of cars. This joint venture ended in 2007. However, with a goal to enter the Chinese market, Fiat found a new partner Guangzhou Automobile Group Co (GAC) and reportedly sold 130,000 cars in China in 2013. Having the right partner with market experience, an extensive supply chain and government support made the difference to Fiat's success in China.

Key Success Factors

1. **A clear partnership vision**
   Establish how a partnership fits within your current business strategy, the anticipated duration, people, and capital requirements as well as the exit expectations. Having laser focused clarity accelerates your ability to create a Partnership Mission statement.

2. **Identification of the right partner**
   Like a marriage, compatibility is a key factor in determining the success of the joint venture. Completing research, interviews and due diligence are all ways to shortlist your ideal partner prior to presenting your Partnerships Vision.

3. **Pitch and plan**
   Create a Partnership Vision pitch deck. With a successful outcome, the joint venture structure, management team, operating assumptions, governance and risk protocols, and financial structure are to be agreed. Having the best team in place to manage the joint venture is key.

4. **Relationship management**
   A successful joint venture is built on trust, communication, and shared goals. Regular effective communication, like any marriage, is key.

The Mantra
"Let's collaborate. We are stronger together."

RICHARD BRANSON, VIRGIN GROUP
The only entrepreneur to build 12 billion dollar companies in 8 sectors

Underperforming at school with dyslexia, at age 16, Richard Branson looked for success in other avenues in life, and channeled his energy into discovering ways to make money. He climbed his way through the ranks from selling Christmas trees and budgerigars to eventually gaining success with a student magazine. The opportunity through this magazine allowed Richard to start undercutting other businesses by selling records cheaper than record shops, and this led him to launch his mail order record business. Following its success, at the age of 22, Richard started a record label, Virgin Records, signing up-and-coming budding artists who were on the rise. Twenty years later, Richard sold Virgin Records to EMI for a reported U.S.D $1 billion, in order to inject funds into his Virgin Atlantic Airways business, founded in 1984, which was coming under fierce competitive pressure from their strong rivals: British Airways.

If you are interested to read more about Richard's fifty year entrepreneur journey with the Virgin Group, it has been well documented. Personally I am a fan of his first book, "Losing my Virginity," which I read as a 19 year old inspiring me to head down the entrepreneur path and "Screw Business as Usual," providing an alternative perspective through a different lens on doing business for good. For the purposes of this book, let's focus on the superpower that I believe led to the rise of the multi-billion dollar Virgin Group.

The Virgin Group consists of over 500 companies, employs 71,000 people in 35 countries and generates U.S.D $20.75 billion annual revenue. Many of the businesses under the Virgin umbrella have succeeded by tapping into the Power of a Partnership. This business model sees Virgin bring the power of its brand name and management team to the table, while the company, typically a leader in its field, brings the infrastructure, people, resources, and knowledge with a shared equity stake.

A prime example of this is how Virgin entered a new sector, Finance, and became the No. 1 Challenger Bank valued at $2.1 billion in 25 years.

In 1994, Richard was keen to disrupt the traditional banking sector by creating a customer centric bank that "made everyone better off." By entering a 50:50 joint venture between Virgin Group and Norwich

Union, Virgin Direct launched offering a tax efficient savings product. The following years, as mortgages and credit cards were added to the product suite, the company changed the name to Virgin Money.

With an energizing vision to one day become a consumer bank, but first requiring a banking license, Virgin Money made a bid for a UK based bank, Northern Rock in 1997; which was unsuccessful. Undeterred by the failure, Richard said *"We will become a bank either by acquisition or by getting our own banking license. You will see us become a consumer bank within the next couple of years."* True to form, Branson was able to bounce back from the failure with a refreshed attitude, and in 2012, Virgin Money acquired Northern Rock, a mortgage lender followed by the Virgin credit card assets managed by MBNA, which is now Bank of America.

In 2019, Clydesdale Bank and Yorkshire Bank (CBYB) bought Virgin Money for $2.1 billion. Interestingly, CBYB dropped its own branding in favor of the more popular global Virgin brand name, which it licenses from Virgin Enterprise. This clearly emphasizes the strength of the brand that Richard had worked hard to create with the use of a clever twenty five year strategy of partnerships and positioning, becoming what is now the 5th largest UK bank.

The Virgin Group has emulated this joint venture strategy multiple times to enter new sectors and territories globally.

Where are They Today?

Sir Richard Branson has a net worth, according to Forbes, of U.S.D $4.6 billion. In 1999, he was knighted by The Queen for his services to entrepreneurism. In 2004, Richard set up Virgin Unite, a philanthropic arm of the Virgin Group, uniting some of the world's greatest leaders, entrepreneurs, voices, and communities to tackle the world's most challenging problems and make a difference by giving back.

Throughout his lifetime, Branson has been searching for new and extreme challenges for him to attempt, and his passion for record breaking adventures continues to this day as he has accomplished many stunning feats, from the fastest Atlantic Ocean crossing to hot air balloon and kitesurfing endeavors. With over 41 million followers and becoming the author of eight books, Branson is heralded as the most social CEO, breaking online records as well. He is part of the billionaire "The Pledge" group and is passionate about space travel, describing Virgin Galactic, the world's first commercial spaceline, as "the greatest adventure of all."

Quote by Richard Branson

"The fundamental driver of our success at Virgin has, and will always be, our people working together. To be successful in business, and in life, you need to connect and collaborate."

BERNIE ECCLESTONE, FORMULA 1
Racing Driver to Billionaire Ringmaster

Bernie Ecclestone's first look into the world of motor sport was as a racing driver at 21 years old. However, his racing career was short lived, due to an incident where he was violently thrown from the car during a crash. Although he emerged unscathed, this near death experience led him to question whether the thrill of racing was really worth putting his life on the line. He duly retired from the sport. But his passion for racing couldn't keep him away for long, and at 27 years old he was drawn back to be in control of the Connaught F1 team, managing their racing drivers, including Stuart Lewis-Evans. Sadly, in the following year, Lewis-Evans crashed and died. Devastated, Bernie walked away from the sport again, shocked by the cruel and brutal horrors of the sport that occurred whilst in chase of the fleeting moments of pure joy. Unfortunately, it was an era that experienced several motorsport deaths as they didn't have the strict safety measures that are in place today.

After years away from Formula One, Bernie was again lured back by the exhilaration of the world of racing, and returned to manage another driver, Jochen Rindt, as well as taking a share in the Lotus Formula 2 team. In the 1970 season, Rindt was killed in a tragic accident during practice for the Italian Grand Prix at Monza. Yet again, a friend had died and he somberly walked away from the sport for the third time.

Bernie's back and forth relationship with F1 continued as in 1971, at the age of 41, he returned and bought the Brabham F1 team for $120,000. Over the next seventeen years, the Brabham team went from strength to strength and Bernie sold the team for $5 million. Bernie had already displayed his shrewd business acumen over the two decades, but it was his ability to harness the power of partnerships that led to him rising to become the Formula One ringmaster, leading to his nickname: the "F1 Supremo."

In the 1970s, the sport was in a shambolic state as there was a big division in the paddock. The teams were split into two camps, the 'Garagistas' consisting of the independent British teams and the "Grandees," the manufacturing giants, Ferrari, Alfa Romeo and Renault. In 1974, the independent teams formed the Formula One Constructors Association (FOCA) to represent their interests against the governing body, the FIA (Federation Internationale de l'Automobile). A strategy of "we are stronger together." At that time, there was an emergence of the commercialization of TV rights as the sport became popular with viewers. Bernie was instrumental in getting appearance money for all the fledgling teams and income from televising Formula One races. In 1978, Bernie became the head of FOCA.

As the global sport continued to grow in popularity with viewers, broadcasters competed to acquire the television rights. In 1987, at the age of 57, Bernie setup Formula One Management (FOM) to manage the Formula 1 rights. With a reputation as an independent team champion coupled with his sharp negotiation skills, Bernie was instrumental in securing the income deal, giving 47% to the teams, 30% to the governing body (FIA), and 23% to himself—Formula One Management.

Where are They Today?

Bernie Eccelstone, now in his nineties, rose from racing driver to ringmaster over a seventy year period. The game changer was when the motorsport strategic alliance was created. In 2019, the scintillating speeds and high octane nature of the sport was enjoyed by 1.9 billion viewers globally, making it one of the world's most popular sports. In 2016, Liberty Media paid $4.4 billion for Formula One Management.

Bernie is a great example of it's never too late to adopt a superpower. Many people retire at 59 years old, yet Bernie pioneering the commercialization of the sport, forging partnerships, and positioning the teams to succeed in an era when the sport was enticing to broadcasters and viewers globally has resulted in his personal net worth of $3.1 billion

Richard Branson and Bernie Eccelestone are not only great examples of the power of a partnership but also that you do not have to keep 100% ownership in order to go from zero to hero.

The Power of Partnership Exercises

"Let's collaborate. We are stronger together."

Do you feel this is your Entrepreneur persona? If so, why? If not, why not? Either answer helps provide insights.

Examples

1. List 3 successful strategic alliances and 3 joint ventures.
2. Summarize the key success factors of these partnerships.

Determine your need

3. Brainstorm 3 reasons why a partnership would fast track your idea/company.
4. What gaps do you currently have? (Sales, distribution, technology, people, etc.)
5. Assess the cost benefits of a partnership.

Discover like-minded companies

6. Now that you have clarity on the WHY, research which companies would be an ideal partner.
7. Seek companies with similar brand values, strategic compatibility, complementary objectives, and cultural fit.

Dive in

8. Contact each company and share your partnership vision plan with them.
9. Outline the WHY first followed by the HOW.
10. Positively share your insights, research, and the financial deal on why you believe you are **STRONGER TOGETHER.**

Join Us

Can you think of other entrepreneurs with this superpower? If you want to meet like minded people or be a contributor sharing real world entrepreneur success stories, please visit www.8superpowers.co.

JOIN the conversation on social media #8superpowers

CATEGORY 4
Method

CHAPTER 7

Power of Process

This chapter focuses on the strategy adopted by entrepreneurs who have simplified the complex through the power of process. Processes are everywhere and in every aspect of our work and leisure. Are some processes more powerful than others?

Before diving into the process strategies, let's look at the problems entrepreneurs face.

1. **Economic Climate**

   We are in a climate that is constantly evolving, with ever increasing disruption, digital transformation of entire industries, increasing protectionism, and pandemics, all at the same time.

2. **Emerging Technologies**

   In 2020, there will be over 30 billion devices connected around the world. Shifts to machine learning and other technologies means human interaction requirements will change. We need to adapt.

3. **Changing Customer Expectations**

   What does the customer of the future look like? Entrepreneurs face the constant challenge of responding to these needs. Many entrepreneurs do not adapt fast enough and fail.

AGILE is the Process Superpower

The two most common approaches during a product development lifecycle are Waterfall and Agile. Waterfall is a linear approach with strict planning and execution step by step with little room for maneuver. This is a less dynamic approach as the project is based on the initial documentation, and the result may not meet the customers' expectations, resulting in additional time and cost after delivery or a product rebuild.

At the other end of the spectrum is Agile, in which a company responds quickly to changes in the economic climate and customer expectations in a productive and cost-effective way without compromising quality. A successful agile entrepreneur displays the perfect blend of an agile mindset, leadership, and management skills. Before we look at the success factors of an agile entrepreneur, what is the agile philosophy?

The Agile Philosophy

Born from frustration in the software development industry in the 1990s, where business and customer expectations were met with cancelled projects and the delayed delivery of technology, a new process improvement method was created. In 2000, seventeen thought leaders founded the Agile Manifesto, which outlines the philosophy, the four core values, and the twelve principles.

Agile is an approach that delivers value more frequently to customers, responds faster to changes, and simplifies the complex. Agile is an iterative approach enabling new features to be added continuously to meet customer requirements; a customer centric approach where change is welcome.

The Four Values of the Agile Manifesto

1. Individuals and interactions over processes and tools
2. Working software over comprehensive documentation
3. Customer collaboration over contract negotiation
4. Responding to change over following a plan

The Twelve Principles

They are the guiding principles for the methodologies.

1. Customer satisfaction through early and continuous software delivery
2. Accommodate changing requirements throughout the development process
3. Frequent delivery of working software
4. Collaboration between business stakeholders and developers throughout the project
5. Support, trust, and motivate people involved
6. Enable face-to-face interactions
7. Working software is the primary measure of progress
8. Agile processes to support a consistent development pace

9. Attention to technical detail and design enhance agility
10. Simplicity
11. Self-organizing teams encourage great architectures, requirement, and designs
12. Regular reflections on how to become more effective

Initially seen as a set of practices relevant to software development, Agile methodologies have become mainstream as companies seek to simplify in the ever-changing, volatile, uncertain, complex, and ambiguous world (VUCA) we live in. Agile enables companies to master continuous change. With the fast pace of technological innovation disrupting industries, many large Fortune 500 companies, IBM, Cisco, and Microsoft, use an Agile approach to improve their processes and adapt quickly to the changes in the market and increase their speed to market. In a survey of 50,000 agile teams by CA Technologies, it was found that Agile can help high-performing teams double their productivity and cut time to market by 50%.

Agile is an attitude, not a technique with boundaries. An attitude has no boundaries, so we wouldn't ask 'can I use agile here', but rather 'how would I act in the agile way here?' or 'how agile can we be here?'

—Alistair Cockburn, co-author of the Agile Manifesto

In today's era of volatility, there is no other way but to re-invent. The only sustainable advantage you can have over others is agility. Because nothing else is sustainable, everything else you create, somebody will replicate.

—Jeff Bezos, Amazon Founder

Success today requires the agility and drive to constantly rethink, reinvigorate, react and reinvent.

—Bill Gates, Microsoft

Innovation is key. Only those who have the agility to change with the market and innovate quickly will survive.

—Robert Kyosakie, Founder Rich Dad

The Rise of the Agile Entrepreneur

Entrepreneurs inherently need to be adaptable to build a successful business. Agile entrepreneurs who have mastered this are not only experts in adopting agile project management tools, like Scrum and Kanban, but experts at leading a team with their agile mindset.

Sue Coyne, an Agile Leadership and Enterprise Coach says,

If an organization focuses only on agile management tools it is very unlikely that it will develop an organization-wide agile culture. Creating an agile culture requires the leaders to embrace an agile mindset, which in turn influences agile leadership behaviors. Their mindset and behaviors will then be imitated by the rest of the organization and an agile culture is created.

Common Agile Methodologies

Scrum, Kanban, Lean Software Development, and Extreme Programming (XP) are all varieties of agile frameworks for product development consistent with the principles in the Agile Manifesto. Let's look at the first two.

1. **Scrum**

    As defined by the co-creators, Ken Schwaber and Jeff Sutherland, Scrum is *"a framework within which people can address complex adaptive problems, while creatively delivering products of the highest possible value."*

    The framework consists of processes and techniques to enable continuous improvement of a product, team, and working environment. Scrum employs an iterative, incremental approach to optimize predictability and control risk. A scrum team is a self-organizing, cross-functional group of people who engage in Sprints, a time boxed development phase, to release incremental product updates. Events like a Daily Scrum (a 15-minute time boxed review and planning session for the development team and a Sprint Retrospective) provide an opportunity for the Scrum Team to inspect itself and adopt lessons into the next Sprint. Written by the methodology founders, The Scrum Guide outlines the values and approach.

2. Kanban

Kanban is a lean method for defining and managing workflow. Kanban is a Japanese term for billboard/signpost. This approach aims to help visualize work in production, facilitate prioritization, and establish bottlenecks. The goal is to create more value for the customer, minimizing waste activities, and maximizing productivity. Kanban was inspired by Toyota, who in the late 1940s, introduced a "just in time" manufacturing method, the Toyota Production System (TPS), to its product development approach. The main tool is the Kanban Board, which has columns of tasks under headings "Requested," "In Progress," and "Done." This results in an agile workflow management process that is often used in conjunction with Scrum.

Agile is the process superpower adopted by many successful companies.

The Mantra
"Let's simplify"

JUDITH FAULKNER
The computer programmer who solved
America's medical data challenge

In the 1970s, fresh off the back of completing her Masters in computer science, a research group in the health industry approached Judith Faulkner as they needed her expertise to create a system to help centralize and keep track of data over time. She wrote the code for a healthcare database management system, which proved highly effective and word was spreading throughout the industry about her innovation, leading to more requests for similar work. The magnitude of her accomplishment was only beginning to be understood as Judith had simplified the complex process of storing medical records for the healthcare sector.

A generous $70,000 investment from friends and family in 1979 propelled her toward co-founding Human Services Computing operating from the basement of the house. The company changed names to Epic Systems and grew slowly over the next decade, securing sixty nine customers by 2000. The company was set up during the Third Revolution, during the rise of the information technology sector where software companies who had cracked the code, simplified a process and packaged it as a software solution could be immensely successful.

Where are They Today?

Epic Systems is America's leading medical record software company, holding over 54% of America's patient records, employing 10,000 people with $2.9 billion in sales. Forbes named Judith Faulkner as "The most successful female technology founder" and a self-made billionaire with a net worth of $3.7 billion.

Judith is a member of The Giving Pledge.

Quote by Judith Faulkner

Many years ago I asked my young children what two things they needed from their parents. They said 'food and money'. I told them 'roots and wings'. My goal in pledging 99% of my assets to philanthropy is to help others with roots—food, warmth, shelter, healthcare, education—so they too can have wings.

One of the things that made Epic strong when I wrote the original code was that it never occurred to me to do anything other than out the patient at the center. I developed a clinical system at a time when the health care world had pretty much only billing and lab systems available.

REED HASTINGS, NETFLIX
A monthly gym membership model revolutionized how the world is entertained

Reed Hastings, another computer programmer, invented a debugging tool for other programmers. The company grew and in 1995, he sold Pure Software for $750 million. Having acquired the taste of success, he was keen to launch another company. Reed Hastings and Marc Randolph brainstormed ideas for a new and groundbreaking business. There are conflicting reports on the inspiration for founding Netflix. For our purposes, we are only interested in the superpower strategy they adopted to become the world's largest streaming service.

Seeking inspiration for a new business, Marc admired the e-commerce model of Amazon of selling books online. He was keen to find something that they could sell and deliver online. DVD's were becoming increasingly popular. After mailing a CD to themselves, arriving intact, they pursued the idea of an online DVD rental store. This fundamentally changed people's buying behavior as you now didn't need to leave your home to watch a movie. They simplified the process of watching entertainment.

The company was the first online DVD rental store with 30 people and 925 titles available to rent. In 1999, the inspiration to move to a subscription based pricing model is said to have come to Reed after receiving a $40 late fee from Blockbuster for a video rental, after a gym visit. The gym membership model is a flat monthly fee regardless of how many times you use it. Netflix adopted a subscription based 'no hidden fees' pricing model, not charging customers late, handling or shipping fees. Yet again they harnessed the concept of simplifying the complex.

The irony is that in 2000, with 300,000 subscribers, Netflix was losing money. Reed offered Netflix to Blockbuster for $50 million. Reed saw it as an online store to complement the traditional retail model. Blockbuster famously turned down the offer. In 2004, Blockbuster had 9000 retail locations. However, this was the third revolution with the Internet economy growing, and in 2005, Netflix had gained 4.5 million subscribers. In 2010, Blockbuster filed for bankruptcy. By 2017, Netflix was valued at $40 billion.

Where are They Today?

A 25 year journey that started as a DVD-by-mail company has evolved into a streaming giant with original content. Over 1 billion hours of content is streamed per week, Netflix has revolutionized the television industry with many companies now following in their wake.

The company's ability to simplify the complex, identify the emergence of trends, pivot, and innovate has kept Netflix at the forefront of the entertainment sector. From the fast spread of DVD players, which saw two thirds of U.S. households have a DVD player in 2002, to the rise of video streaming services, combined with the streaming bandwidth rapidly improving, has enabled Netflix to become the unicorn company it is today. Netflix employees over 8000 people, has 183 million customers, which generated $20 billion revenue in 2019, making it the world's largest online subscription video service.

The rise of Netflix is well documented by both Founders in their books, *"No Rules Rules - Netflix and the Culture of Reinvention"* by Reed Hastings attributes the unique culture to successfully scaling the business. His experience with a dysfunctional culture at his first startup company led him to be passionate about cracking the culture code the second time around. His belief is that to succeed, you have to leverage every person in the organization and have an intentional culture. The original Netflix Culture Deck has received over 10 million views on SlideShare. Marc Randolph's book *"That Will Never Work: The Birth of Netflix"* is also worth reading.

A passionate philanthropist with a net worth of $3.6 billion, Reed is part of the Giving Pledge community. Marc Randolph left Netflix in 2002, once it went public, knowing his passion lay in helping startups scale. *"At the beginning, it's very much triage. If there are a hundred things broken and you need the skill to pick the three you've got to fix, I'm really good at that. I'm not good at the other ninety-seven."* Randolph said. Also a philanthropist and environmentalist, Randolph supports 1% for the Planet, a global movement to bring together "dollars and doers to accelerate smart environmental giving."

Quotes by Reed Hastings

I got the idea for Netflix after my company was acquired. I had a big late fee for Apollo 13. It was six weeks late and I owed the video store $40. I had misplaced the cassette. It was all my fault.

Companies rarely die from moving too fast, and they frequently die from moving too slowly.

I learned the value of focus. I learned it is better to do one product well than two products in a mediocre way.

There are many notable entrepreneurs that could feature in this section. I have chosen to showcase two companies disrupting the Finance sector, one of the most traditional, regulated sectors of all.

In 2017, Anne Boden, a seasoned finance sector expert, saw the opportunity to harness the power of the fourth revolution to disrupt the traditional banking sector. Starling Bank is Britain's first non-retail, App only mobile bank and has 1 million customers with $1.25 billion in deposits. Traditional banks have high street outlets manned with people to meet the needs of the customer. Starling Bank has simplified the process, cutting out the retail presence and associated overhead costs, existing solely as an App only mobile bank. A multi-award winning business model that continues to grow from strength to strength.

Also noteworthy are entrepreneurs, Nicolas Storonksy and Vlad Yatsenko who re-invented the way we spend and transfer money abroad. As an avid traveler, Nicolas was frustrated with wasting money on foreign transactions fees and exchange rate commissions charged by traditional companies. He envisioned a multi-currency card with no hidden fees, transparent on all commission charges. They found a way to simplify the complex. Revolut launched in 2015 and has acquired 10 million users with a Banking-as-a-Service model where customers are happy to pay a monthly subscription for its services.

The Power of Process Exercises

"Let's Simplify"

Do you feel this is your Entrepreneur persona? If so, why? If not, why not? Either answer helps provide insights.

1. Discover if you have an agile mindset. Visit www.8superpower. co to take the test.
2. Complete a customer journey map for your product/service.
3. Assess how many steps it takes end to end.
4. Complete a ruthless prioritization exercise to rank which steps are essential and non-essential.
5. Brainstorm 5 ways you can simplify the process.
6. Create an experiment to test the new process. Be agile. Test. Learn. Adapt. Repeat.
7. Learn about agile principles, exercises, and tools (like Kanban, Scrum).
8. List 5 ways you could simplify your home, work, and personal life.

Join Us

Can you think of other entrepreneurs with this superpower? If you want to meet like minded people or be a contributor sharing real world entrepreneur success stories, please visit www.8superpowers.co.

JOIN the conversation on social media #8superpowers

CATEGORY 5

Movement

CHAPTER 8

Power of Planet

What is a Social Enterprise?

A social enterprise is an organization whose mission combines revenue growth and profit making with the need to respect and support its environment and stakeholder network. This includes listening to, investing in, and actively managing the trends that are shaping today's world. It is an organization that shoulders its responsibility to be a good citizen (both inside and outside the organization), serving as a role model for its peers and promoting a high degree of collaboration at every level of the organization.

as defined by Deloitte.

Bill Drayton, founder of Ashoka, is considered the grandfather of social entrepreneurism. He believes that the most powerful force for good in the world is a social entrepreneur: a person driven by innovative ideas that can help correct an entrenched global problem. Ashoka envisions a world in which everyone is a changemaker.

The Socially Conscious Movement

In today's connected world, financial performance is not enough as companies are increasingly being judged on how they treat their people, partnerships, and the impact they are having on the planet.

The key drivers of this movement are:

1. **Millennials**

   Millennials believe their children will grow up in a world worse than their parents unless change happens. The awareness of social issues around the globe is harder to ignore, from wars, poverty, plastic waste, disasters, and environmental challenges being reported daily.

2. **Trust**

   Since the global financial crisis, this movement has been driven by social, economic, and political change where people are increasingly relying on companies to take the lead on social and environmental issues as opposed to governments. In 2018, the Edehan Trust Barometer reported that 52% place trust in business "to do what is right" versus 43% trust in government. Citizens are looking for businesses to deal with key issues.

3. **Ecosystem maturity**

   With entrepreneur ecosystems growing globally, it is easier for a social entrepreneur to tap into a network of investors, incubators, mentors, and like-minded people and gain the resources required to be successful. Ashoka is one of the most successful social entrepreneur networks with 3,300 social entrepreneurs in 88 countries tackling the world's most pressing problems.

Social Enterprise Business Models

By selling goods and services in the open market, a social impact business aims to create employment, make a profit, and reinvest or donate to create positive social change. Social enterprises exist across sectors, from consumer goods to healthcare. Doing business for good is at the heart of the business model. There are several strategies adopted; here are my top three.

1. **One for One**

   TOMS is the original One for One company. When you buy a pair of TOMS shoes, one pair goes to a person in need. The socially conscious giving movement has led to a rise in this buy-one-give-one model.

   - The One World Play Project is a social impact company that creates ultra-durable balls to enable play for everyone, everywhere in the world. To date, more than 2 million unpoppable soccer balls have been delivered to 185 countries, impacting an estimated 60 million people.
   - Smile Squared donates a toothbrush to a child in need with every purchase.
   - SoapBox, started by a college student in 2010, has donated more than one million donations.

- Fighting for literacy, Better World Books, "Book for Book" scheme has donated more than 26 million books and raised more than $18 million for global literacy and local libraries.

2. **Pay It Forward**

This approach seeks to attract people who enjoy a service and enable others to have the same experience. Mason Wartman left his Wall Street job to open a pay-it-forward pizza company in Philadelphia, one of United States' worst poverty rate cities suffering homelessness. The concept launched after he bought a slice and wrote a Post-it note on the wall inviting the next homeless person who entered to redeem the offer. Since the first pay-it-forward slice, Rosa's has provided nearly 10,000 pizza slices to needy Philadelphians. One of his homeless regulars found a job and sought to pay it forward as others had done for him.

Another inspiring example is Daniel Lubetzky, founder of KIND Snacks, who since 2004 has been on a mission to make the world a little kinder one snack and act at a time. The KIND movement has inspired 5 million acts of kindness.

3. **Contribution**

Founded in 1991, The Big Issue is one of the UK's leading social businesses offering homeless people the opportunity to earn an income. Vendors buy The Big Issue magazine for £1.50 and sell it for £3 meaning each seller is a micro-entrepreneur who is working, not begging. In the past 25 years, 92,000 vendors have earned £115 million by selling over 200 million copies. This award winning publication has inspired over 120 similar magazines in 35 countries.

ME to WE, ranked by Forbes as one of the top 5 most successful and impactful social enterprises of this generation, uses technology to enable consumers to track exactly how and where the funds from their Fairtrade products are changing lives. This high level transparency enables the buyer to see where their contribution is making a difference.

I too embrace a social entrepreneur approach. The 8 Superpowers is not just a book, it is an impact brand that seeks to make a difference in the world through books and courses. The 8 Superpowers tribe is passionate about learning and chooses to empower those less fortunate with an education.

As I mentioned in the introduction, the royalties from book sales are donated to Pencils of Promise (PoP), a non-profit organization that builds schools and increases educational opportunities in the developing world. Pencils of Promise believe where you start in life shouldn't dictate where you finish. In partnership with local governments and communities, PoP continues to provide students with access to safe primary schools, implement proven programs, and invest in teacher quality. To date, Pencils of Promise has built 530 schools globally, supported 2,151 teachers, and impacted 110,380 students.

The 8 Superpowers brand is on a mission to empower those less fortunate with an education. 250 million children lack basic reading, writing, and math skills. As Nelson Mandela said, "Education is the most powerful weapon you can use to change the world." My vision is to raise the $50,000 required to build an entire school. If you are interested in participating, please join the 8 Superpowers community via the website. We are stronger together.

Top 5 Success Factors for Impact Businesses

As doing business for good is at the heart of a social enterprise, these five factors are key to its success.

1. **An impact mission statement**
   Most businesses have a mission statement, however, it is of utmost importance that an impact business has clarity on the change it seeks to make in the world in order to attract the right people, partners, and investors.

   Example mission statements from impact brands are:

   - Alter Eco Foods—Our mission is global transformation through ethical relationships with small-scale farmers, and an integral sustainability orientation at every point on the supply chain.

- AltSchool—We believe every child should have access to an exceptional, personalized education that enables them to be happy and successful in an ever-changing world.
- Cradles to Crayons: Provides children from birth through to age 12, living in homeless or low-income situations, with the essential items they need to thrive—at home, at school, and at play.
- Feronia Forests is dedicated to finding smart ways to nurture, improve, and conserve forestland for future generations.
- No One Without—To overcome death and disease resulting from the consumption of contaminated water by providing safe, clean water to those in need around the world.
- Tesla—To accelerate the world's transition to sustainable energy.
- TED—Spread ideas.

How does a Mission Statement Vary from a Vision Statement?

A mission statement clarifies what, who, and the why of a company whereas a vision statement is the outcome of the successful implementation of the mission; the impact the company will have on the world.

Vision statement examples:

- TOMS: The responsibility of providing for the comfort of children in impoverished regions worldwide.
- Grameen Bank: A world free of poverty.

2. **Manage the ecosystem**

   Actively manage your position in the social ecosystem by engaging with key stakeholders, from governments to regulatory bodies, educational institutions, and communities. Create an ecosystem map to understand the key players and how you fit into the puzzle to solve the problem. Reach out to all relevant participants within the ecosystem and share your mission to unlock opportunities.

3. **Collaborate**

   Social enterprise C suites regularly collaborate on long term interdependent work. 33% are more likely to expect companies to grow at 10% or more during the next year compared to the leaders who operate independently, according to the Deloitte Human Global Human Capital Trends Report.

4. **Enable a blended work-life approach**

The lines between work and life have blurred further since the coronavirus pandemic with activities like remote working and educating children at home eating into the traditional 9 am to 5 pm work schedule. Social entrepreneurs seek flexibility to make a difference on their own terms at their own pace, whenever, wherever.

5. **The Impact statement**

It is crucial to measure the value and benefit a social business is having on people, communities, and the planet. Be bold. Share it.

The TOMS website has a dedicated "Impact" page stating:

We're in business to improve lives. TOMS has always stood for a better tomorrow - one where humanity thrives. To us, that means no matter who you are or where you live, you feel physically safe, mentally healthy, and have equal access to opportunity. Every TOMS purchase enables us to invest in local partners around the world who are working to create positive change in these three areas.

- 13 years of giving
- 96.5 million lives impacted
- 780,000 sight restorations
- 722,000 weeks of safe water
- $6.5 million committed in impact grants
- Given in 85 countries
- 205 giving partners onboard

The ME to WE Impact Statement:

- $20 million in cash and cost-offsetting in-kind donations to WE charity
- 12,000 partner retail stores that carry ME to WE or Track Your Impact products

- 10 million social impacts funded and delivered through product purchases
- 42,000 travelers to communities around the world to volunteer on development projects and see the impacts first hand
- 140,000 students receive leadership training annually
- 86% of ME to WE management level staff are female

Impact statements engage and empower your audience to be part of the movement.

The Mantra
"Be the change you want to see in the world"

ANITA RODDICK, BODY SHOP
Cruelty free products changed the face of retail

In 1976, Anita Roddik opened a small store—The Body Shop—that sold natural-ingredient cosmetics on the basic, but at that time, a revolutionary principle that no products were tested on animals. This coupled with an ahead of their time green-minded recycling policy, after urine sample bottles ran out and were refilled, led to the rise of a tribe of consumers with the ethos of social responsibility and environmental change. In the 1970s, testing cosmetic ingredients on animals was the norm, until Anita provided consumers with a choice. Anita's green values and business model showed there was another way to do business for good while making a profit; profits with principles. As a keen activist and campaigner with great business acumen, Anita opened another store within a year and subsequently rolled out the franchising model, which appealed to the like-minded socio-ethical entrepreneurs keen to be part of the green movement.

By 1984, The Body Shop had 138 stores. In 1987, Anita's stance against animal cruelty championed the ethical sourcing of ingredients from underdeveloped countries leading to the Trade Not Aid program. The Body Shop partnered with struggling communities and purchased their unique ingredients for their products, such as Brazil nut oil from the Kayapo Indians of the Amazon River Basin, thereby helping communities thrive and earn a livelihood. As more community based programs rolled out globally, Anita became the First Lady of the Fair Trade movement and is recognized as the pioneer that changed the face of retail.

By 2000, sixteen years later, the number of stores had exponentially boomed to 2000 in 50 countries. The powerful combination of products (cruelty free), ingredients (ethically sourced), marketing (storytelling) and passionate consumers who align with these values, led to a successful business that was acquired by L'Oreal in 2006 for $1.14 billion.

Where are They Today?

At the age of 19, I read Anita Roddick's book, "Body and Soul: Profits with Principles." This was my first entrepreneur autobiography and gave me insights into a world of passion, meaning, philanthropy, and making money whilst also crucially making a difference to the world. Sadly, my role model, Anita Roddick passed away at the age of 64. Her famous quote *"If you do things well, do them better. Be daring, be first, be different, be just"* lives with me today.

Anita uniquely combined her activism with her business acumen to create a global company, and not only changed the face of ethical consumerism but also hit a major milestone for her personally when animal testing was banned in the UK in 1997 and then the European Union in 2009. Her legacy lives on.

Today there are social and environmental campaigners, from the young to the old. Greta Thunberg, a teenage climate activist, created a global movement, Fridays for Future, a school strike to raise awareness of climate change. For me, when you combine that level of passion with business acumen you truly can be "the change you want to see in the world."

Quotes by Anita Roddick

"If you think you are too small to have an impact, try going to bed with a mosquito in the room."

"The business of business should not just be about money, it should be about responsibility. It should be about public good, not private greed."

MUHAMMED YANUS, GRAMEEN BANK
A University Research Project Led to the World's Largest Trust Based Bank for the Poor

In 1974, Economics Professor Muhammed Yanus organized a student field trip to a local village in Bangladesh, where he encountered a woman making bamboo stools. Keen to discover the economics enabling the activity, he learnt she had borrowed money to buy the raw bamboo materials and after repaying the middleman, it did not leave enough profit to raise the woman above the subsistence levels. Following this insight, Muhammed, as a research project, chose to lend $27 to 42 basket weavers, and made $0.02 on each loan.

With roots growing up in a village himself, coupled with his mother's selfless inspirational actions by helping everyone she could, Yanus was inspired to eradicate poverty in the villages of Bangladesh. In 1983, he set up the village bank—Grameen Bank—on the foundational belief that the poor know best where their own income should be spent and loans have better outcomes than charitable donations. Even small amounts would allow them a critical head start and a chance for a brighter future. Providing a loan would enable them to bring their ideas to life, earn a regular income: a more sustainable model to raise them from poverty. A unique business model helped many people toward upward social mobility through entrepreneurial endeavors.

Grameen Bank was the first collateral free community bank to microfinance loans to the poor. With no contracts, the core values—the Sixteen Decisions—is what drives the success of the community trust based model, which experiences the highest repayment rate of any banking system.

Where are They Today?

Grameen Bank has over 2600 branches, 9 million borrowers, 97% are women with an exceptional 99.6% repayment rate. The success led to other projects in 64 countries emulating the successful social business model. Grameen Bank has expanded its loan programs to other areas, from phones to housing.

Muhammed Yanus is one of the greatest social entrepreneurs who pioneered the micro-lending movement enabling millions of people to get out of poverty. In recognition for his work, he has been awarded over 50 honorary degrees, 113 international awards from 26 countries, the Nobel Peace Prize, and dozens of books and movies about his work.

Quotes By Muhammed Yanus

All human beings are born entrepreneurs. Some get a chance to unleash that capacity. Some never got the chance, never knew that he or she has that capacity'.

Human creativity is unlimited. It is the capacity of humans to make things happen which didn't happen before. Creativity provides the key to solving our social and economic problems.'

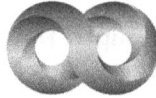

BLAKE MYCOSKIE, TOMS SHOES
A village visit resulted in 100 million pairs of shoes gifted

After visiting a village in Argentina where children in extreme poverty couldn't afford shoes, socially minded entrepreneur Blake Mycoskie founded TOMS Shoes. He had enjoyed a mildly successful career with five businesses previously, however, this business started as a result of a passion to solve the problem and gained fast success as a result of the unique philanthropic approach that appealed to shoe buyers.

Blake's "One for One" concept was a game changer model that became popular with consumers in every avenue of life. Today, it sounds simple "help one person with every purchase," however, no one had executed this strategy as successfully before or expanded it to other retail categories. For every coffee purchased, it provides a week of clean water, for every eyewear purchased a person's eyesight is restored. Attracting a tribe of like-minded socially conscious people has led to 100 million shoes being gifted, 600,000 eyesights restored and 600,000 weeks of safe water for under-privileged people.

Blake's book "Start Something That Matters" is worth a read if the Power of the Planet is the superpower strategy you identify with.

Quotes by Blake Mycoskie

The most important step of all is the first step. Start something.

If you organize your life around your passion, you can turn your passion into your story and then turn your story into something bigger—something that matters.

I believe each of us has a mission in life, and that one cannot truly be living their most fulfilled life until they recognise this mission and dedicate their life to pursuing it.

Entrepreneurs tapping into this superpower are the ones that have created a whole new business model that has social and environmental impacts. Whether it is Anita Roddick's Fairtrade model, Yanus microlending to the poor, or Blake Mycoskie's One for One concept, this type of entrepreneur embodies the change they want to see in the world.

The Power of Planet Exercises

"Be the change you want to see in the world"

Do you feel this is your Entrepreneur persona? If so, why? If not, why not? Either answer helps provide insights.

1. What problem do you want to solve and why?
2. Write a mission statement outlining who you want to serve and how you will serve them.
3. What will your purpose driven product/service do?
4. Complete research on who your competitors may be and how they are changing the world.
5. Develop a one page social enterprise business model that fits your concept outlining how your social enterprise will generate money as well as being of service to others.
6. List 3 social entrepreneurs you admire and why.
7. Get a roadmap from successful social entrepreneurs. Contact or study them. Ask:
   a. If you could do it differently next time, what would you do?
   b. List the top 3 reasons why you think you succeeded?
   c. What advice would you give to a budding social entrepreneur?

Join Us

Can you think of other entrepreneurs with this superpower? If you want to meet like minded people or be a contributor sharing real world entrepreneur success stories, please visit www.8superpowers.co.

JOIN the conversation on social media #8superpowers

CHAPTER 9

Power of the 8 P's

Putting It All Together

This book showcases the primary strategies adopted by successful entrepreneurs. Imagine if, as well as a primary strategy being adopted, all the eight strategies were implemented simultaneously, in a defined time period.

The 8P's is a framework for building and growing companies by adopting eight strategies and their associated approaches simultaneously. This book has showcased the primary strategy adopted by highly successful entrepreneurs. By adopting all 8 superpower strategies simultaneously maximizes an entrepreneurs opportunity to succeed.

The 8 P's Goals

After years of research studying the strategies of successful entrepreneurs, the 8P Method was created to bring the insights in a simple, adoptable approach for anyone seeking to maximize their business success. Whether you are a student, existing entrepreneur, or an experienced professional, the 8P's aim to inspire you to try one, a combination, or all eight superpower strategies simultaneously and see the results.

The 8 P's Method

The framework consists of five pillars, eight strategies, and twenty approaches to facilitate strategic clarity, implementation, and execution. Each component has a proven outcome with demonstrable case studies to highlight its effectiveness.

The 5 Categories

The strategies fall into five categories—the 5 M's.

    Category 1—MINDSET—Problem and Perseverance
    Category 2—MARKETING—Positioning and Proximity
    Category 3—MASSES—People and Partnerships
    Category 4—METHOD—Process
    Category 5—MOVEMENT—Planet

The 8P's Framework

CATEGORIES	Category 1 MINDSET	Category 2 MARKETING	Category 3 MASSES	Category 4 METHOD	Category 5 MOVEMENT

CATEGORY 1: MINDSET

Superpower 1: Problem

The Mantra
"I'm driven to create something new to solve the problem."

Entrepreneurs with a problem solving mindset are driven to create solutions. Products are used daily that trigger thoughts like, *"this would be better if…."* and *"if only this was faster…"* yet the majority of us accept the status quo. There are a minority who decide to take action, create and launch a new product. What drives these entrepreneurs? Do they have a unique outlook and approach?

The problem solving approaches are:

1. **Algorithms**
   Algorithms simplify the complex by using step-by-step instructions that will produce the same result every time they are performed. The earliest algorithm recorded was in Babylonian times, 1600 BC, on a clay tablet, an early form of an instruction manual to solve a class of problems. Today, the most famous publicized algorithm is PageRank, Google's algorithm to rank the pages on the search engine, created by Larry Page and Sergey Brin while studying at Stanford University.

2. **Heuristics**
   Heuristics, derived from Greek word meaning "to discover," uses shortcuts to produce good-enough solutions in a given timeframe.

They enable quick decisions particularly when working with complex data. You may solve the problem through trial and error, having an educated guess, or using rule of thumb thinking.

3. **Insights**

   Defined as the moment of sudden comprehension of a problem and the solution is often accompanied by an aha experience (Ollinger et al. 2013). Researchers say that an insight occurs because you realize that the problem is actually similar to something you have dealt with in the past. In most cases, the underlying mental processes that lead to insight happen outside of awareness.

Superpower 2: Perseverance

The Mantra
"I will keep trying until I succeed."

Perseverance is the ability to keep doing something in spite of the obstacles. People who persevere show steadfastness in doing something despite how hard or how long it takes. A superpower that combines self-belief, tenacity, and determination above and beyond the average person coupled with an immunity to the fear of failure. This mindset can be defined as resilience, grit, and hard work over a period of time despite recurring failures.

The Perseverance Approach is:

4. **Growth Mindset**

   Can you develop perseverance? Of course! Carol Dweck, Ph.D., a psychology professor at Stanford University, has spent her career studying motivation and achievement. In her book, Mindset: The New Psychology of Success, she presents the difference between a fixed mindset and a growth mindset. A fixed mindset believes their most basic abilities can be developed through dedication and hard work and view their limitations as permanent. A growth mindset interprets challenges and failures as opportunities for personal growth with no boundaries or limitations. Virtually all great people have a growth mindset.

CATEGORY 2: MARKETING

Superpower 3: Positioning

The Mantra
"I will boldly go where no-one has been before."

Positioning refers to the place a brand resides in the minds of customers. A positioning strategy is when an entrepreneur identifies a key area to excel in to gain competitive advantage.

Key Positioning Approaches:

5. **Cost positioning** focuses on ways to eliminate costly procedures in order to pass the savings onto the customer.
6. **Quality positioning** relies on becoming known for using high quality materials, parts, and suppliers enabling a higher price tag due to excellent materials and performance.
7. **Flexibility positioning** embraces the ability to change products and services based on customers' changing needs. Introducing new products to meet changing buying needs requires agility, foresight, and vision.
8. **Speed positioning** allows companies to compete by delivering their product and services quickly to their customers.
9. **Price positioning** is the approach you take to set the price of the products and services you sell. It requires research, calculations, data, and an understanding of different market factors—like your competitors, consumers ability to pay, market conditions, trade margins, and operating costs. The right pricing strategy gives you the ability to maximize profit.

Superpower 4: Proximity

Imagine if you can be successful simply by being in close proximity to the right people in the right place. Would you move to a new city to immerse yourself into an ecosystem to maximize your success?

Originally proposed by social psychologist, Leon Festinger in the 1950s, the proximity or propinquity effect is the idea that physical and/or psychological closeness increases familiarity and attraction. A tendency for people to form friendships with those they encounter more often. According to psychologist Theodore Newcomb, proximity promotes readiness of communication, as a result of which, individuals have an opportunity to discover each other's common attitudes.

The key proximity approaches are:

10. **People Proximity**

Research by Harvard social psychologist Dr. David McClelland demonstrated that the people you habitually associate with determine as much as 95 percent of your success or failure in life.

11. **Place Proximity**

Place proximity can be seen in effect at both macro and micro levels. The Power of Proximity chapter provides detailed insights into these.

CATEGORY 3: MASSES

Superpower 5: People

The Mantra
"I want to be like you, teach me"

The key People approaches are:

12. **Mirror Mentors**

Mentors offer personal support and advice to entrepreneurs, not the broader company. Advisors work on behalf of the company and its shareholders. By having a mentor who has "been there, seen it, and done it!" acting as a sounding board enables the entrepreneur to share the peaks and troughs of building a business with a trusted person. Mentors can exist in many forms; a mentor can be a role model who an entrepreneur may want to emulate, or they may be someone who has created a step by step guide and laid out the path to success in a book and course, or someone who regularly speaks to the entrepreneur. Most successful entrepreneurs can tell you who was their first mentor and how they helped to inspire them to follow their path and maximize their capabilities.

13. **Beef up the Board**

A confident entrepreneur with heightened self-awareness seeks to hire more experienced people than themselves to gain credibility and accelerate company growth faster. This strategy satisfies investors and customers as the company appears highly professional, capable and robust. Engagement of their services may be immersive or infrequent depending on what the startup can afford at that time or the company's growth phase, from seed to Series B.

This approach is now widely used in the startup ecosystem resulting in a new trend for companies to hire in Advisory Panels. But crucially, they are not mentors to the executive team or employees of the company, they only advise. The typical advisory topics range from business expertise in strategy and business development to sector specific expertise in media, legal, medical, for example. Often a seasoned Advisor brings their wealth of experience to 5–10 startups at a time thereby creating a "Portfolio Career." It is a win-win for both the entrepreneur and the advisor.

14. **Community Building**

"I will create a tribe to succeed"

Building a loyal tribe of brand evangelists is a powerful yet underutilized success strategy. Attracting like-minded people passionate about your cause, building trust, and empowering them with the tools to broadcast the brand message to their followers requires vision, planning, and time. To build a community you have to stand for something, be a champion that moves people to follow your vision.

Superpower 6: Partnerships

There are many reasons companies choose to collaborate, from leveraging each other's expertise to entering a new market or territory.

A partnership

- Fuels innovation
- Decreases costs as a result of pooling resources
- Increases productivity

- Instant gain in people, infrastructure, culture, regulation
- Achieves rapid strategic growth
- Offers access to both local and distant markets
- Economies of scale and market power

The key partnership approaches are:

15. **Strategic Alliance**

   Strategic alliances are on the rise. According to PwC, 48 percent of global CEO's planned to pursue a strategic alliance in 2019. In a continually unstable economic climate, a strategic partnership can help drive corporate growth and help companies win. It is a collaborative agreement between two or more companies that come together for a mutually beneficial goal while remaining separate entities. Some alliances provide organizations with a new set of skills or capabilities, others seek the opportunity to cross sell products into a new customer base. They are an alternative to the organic option of building a new business from the ground up, or the organic option of making an acquisition. The strategic alliance is planned and executed by representatives of both companies.

16. **Joint Venture**

   A joint venture is the next level in which two or more businesses sign a contractual agreement thereby creating a third, jointly owned company sharing in the profit and losses. Typically, a new management team oversees the joint venture.

CATEGORY 4: METHOD

Superpower 7: Process

Processes are everywhere and in every aspect of our work and leisure. What if some processes are more powerful than others?

   The key process approach is:

17. **Agile**

   The two most common approaches during a product development lifecycle are Waterfall and Agile. Waterfall is a linear approach with strict planning and execution step by step with little room for maneuvering. A less dynamic approach as the project is based on the initial documentation, and the result may not meet the customers' expectations, resulting in additional time and cost after delivery or a product rebuild.

At the other end of the spectrum is Agile in which a company responds quickly to changes in the economic climate and customer expectations in a productive and cost-effective way without compromising quality. A successful agile entrepreneur displays the perfect blend of an agile mindset, leadership, and management skills.

The Agile Philosophy

Born from frustration in the software development industry in the 1990s, where business and customer requirements were not met by the delivery of technology on time and cancelled projects, a new process improvement method was created. In 2000, seventeen thought leaders founded the Agile Manifesto, which outlines the philosophy, the four core values and twelve principles.

Agile is an approach that delivers value more frequently to customers, responds faster to changes, and simplifies the complex. Agile is an iterative approach enabling new features to be added continuously to meet customer requirements. A customer centric approach where change is welcome.

CATEGORY 5: MOVEMENT

Superpower 8: Planet

"A social enterprise is an organization whose mission combines revenue growth and profit making with the need to respect and support its environment and stakeholder network. This includes listening to, investing in, and actively managing the trends that are shaping today's world. It is an organization that shoulders its responsibility to be a good citizen (both inside and outside the organization), serving as a role model for its peers and promoting a high degree of collaboration at every level of the organization." as defined by Deloitte.

The Socially Conscious Movement

In today's connected world, financial performance is not enough as companies are increasingly being judged on how they treat their people, partnerships and the impact they are having on the planet. By selling goods and services in the open market, a social impact business aims to create employment, make a profit, and reinvest or donate to create positive social change. Social enterprises exist across sectors, from consumer goods to healthcare. Doing business for good is at the heart of the business model.

The key Planet approaches are:

18. **One for One**

    TOMS is the original One for One company. When you buy a pair of TOMS shoes, one pair goes to a person in need. The socially conscious giving movement has led to a rise in this buy-one-give-one model.

19. **Pay It Forward**

    This approach seeks to attract people who enjoy a service and enable others to have the same experience. Mason Wartman left his Wall Street job to open a pay-it-forward pizza company in Philadelphia, one of United States' worst poverty rate cities suffering homelessness. The concept launched after he bought a slice and wrote a Post-it note on the wall inviting the next homeless person who entered to redeem the offer. Since the first pay-it-forward slice, Rosa's has provided nearly 10,000 pizza slices to needy Philadelphians. One of his homeless regulars found a job and sought to pay it forward as others had done for him.

20. **Contribution**

    Founded in 1991, The Big Issue is one of the UK's leading social businesses offering homeless people the opportunity to earn an income. Vendors buy The Big Issue magazine for £1.50 and sell it for £3 meaning each seller is a micro-entrepreneur who is working, not begging. In the past 25 years, 92,000 vendors have earned £115 million by selling over 200 million copies. This award winning publication has inspired over 120 similar magazines in 35 countries.

How to implement and execute the 8P Method

"Strategy is important, but execution is everything."

—Jeff Haden

"Execution is the ability to mesh strategy with reality, align people with goals, and achieve the promised results"

—Lawrence Bossidy

There are several successful implementation and execution methods around. Methods that keep you on track, accountable and moving forward. To keep this toolkit current it lives on the website.

What's Next?

The Community

If you have enjoyed this book and you would like to explore, inspire and meet like minded people, join the Community. Its free!

Our mission is to help entrepreneurs to overcome the odds, share best practices success stories and champion impact entrepreneurs. As a member, you'll get access to live sessions and the latest case studies. Visit www.8superpowers.co to learn more

Become a Certified 8Ps Method Coach

Be personally trained by Marina Nicholas to become a Certified 8Ps Method Coach to become a highly sought after business coach helping businesses grow.

Regardless of your experience with coaching, becoming a certified 8P Method Coach will give you the strategies, toolkit and confidence to take your coaching to the next level. Join Marina on a quest to inspire and impact the world by becoming an accredited Certified Coach. You will gain a deep understanding of the 8P framework, the 5 categories, 8 superpower strategies and 20 approaches. Interactive group sessions will guide you on how to deliver the 8Ps Method to any business, from startups to large enterprises, successfully.

You can study from anywhere in the world, online, at your own pace. Visit www.8superpowers.co for more information.

References

Introduction

https://weforum.org/agenda/2016/01/what-is-the-fourth-industrial-revolution/
https://abcnews.go.com/Business/half-worlds-entire-wealth-hands-millionaires/story?id=66440320
https://betterexplained.com/articles/how-to-develop-a-sense-of-scale/
https://forbes.com/sites/hanktucker/2020/05/03/coronavirus-bankruptcy-tracker-these-major-companies-are-failing-amid-the-shutdown/#38761653425a
https://ft.com/content/9c9d1ec2-8898-11ea-a109-483c62d17528
https://get2growth.com/how-many-startups/

Chapter 1—Problem

https://verywellmind.com/problem-solving-2795008
https://frontiersin.org/articles/10.3389/fpsyg.2019.00002/full
https://frontiersin.org/articles/10.3389/fpsyg.2017.00827/full
Jung-Beeman, M, E.M. Bowden, J. Haberman J.L. Frymiare, S. Arambel-Liu, R. Greenblatt, P.J. Reber, J. Kounios. April 2004. "Neural Activity When People Solve Verbal Problems with Insight." *PLOS Biology* (published 2004) 2, no. 4, p. E97.
https://famousscientists.org/7-great-examples-of-scientific-discoveries-made-in-dreams/
https://mentalfloss.com/article/12763/11-creative-breakthroughs-people-had-their-sleep
https://spanx.com/about-us
https://muchneeded.com/airbnb-statistics/
https://bloomberg.com/news/articles/2018-02-06/inside-airbnb-s-battle-to-stay-private
"The World's 100 Most Powerful Women." *Forbes. Forbes. Retrieved 26 June 2014*
Statt, N. February 3, 2020. "YouTube is a $15 Billion-a-Year Business, Google Reveals for the First Time." *The Verge.* Retrieved February 3, 2020
"Alphabet Announces Fourth Quarter and Fiscal Year 2019 Results" (PDF) (Press release). *Alphabet Inc. February 3, 2020.* Retrieved February 3, 2020.
Picker, L. June 25, 2014. "GoPro Touts Media Ahead of IPO for Higher Value Than Cameras." *Bloomberg.* Retrieved July 22, 2001

https://gopro.com/en/gb/about-us

https://philanthropynewsdigest.org/news/gopro-founders-donate-500-million-to-community-foundation

https://investor.gopro.com/press-releases/press-release-details/2019/GoPro-Announces-Second-Quarter-2019-Results/

https://fortunly.com/statistics/startup-statistics/#gref

"Ben & Jerry's Location Count." *Entrepreneur*. Retrieved January 23, 2020.

Chapter 2—Perseverance

http://jkrowling.com/wp-content/uploads/2020/03/JKR.com-media-kit-biog.pdf

https://qz.com/961875/how-jk-rowling-overcame-depression-and-rejection-to-end-up-selling-400-million-books/

https://entrepreneur.com/article/323363

https://thalesgroup.com/en/worldwide/group/case-study/top-10-inventors-all-time

Chapter 3—Positioning

https://corporate.walmart.com/our-story/our-history

https://amazon.com/dp/B07PQ67F55/ref=cm_sw_em_r_mt_dp_U_pJ2JCbZ4XACTC

Walmart Investor Relations - Investors - Financial Information - Unit Counts & Square Footage." *stock.walmart.com*. Retrieved February 18, 2020.

Featherstone, L. November 21, 2005. "Wal-Mart Charity Evaluated: Critics Question Company's Motives." *The Nation. Archived from the Original on October 29, 2013*. Retrieved August 1, 2013

"Sunday Times Rich List." *thesundaytimes.co.uk*.

https://gatesfoundation.org/who-we-are/general-information/foundation-factsheet

Chapter 4—Proximity

https://thedrum.com/opinion/2020/03/16/how-proximity-marketing-can-help-the-high-street

https://blog.beaconstac.com/2016/02/25-retailers-nailing-it-with-their-proximity-marketing-campaigns/

https://cpbml.org.uk/news/motorsport-valley-centre-manufacturing-excellence

http://bulovacorporatesalesblog.com/productivity-and-goal-setting/performance-proximity-high-performers-boost-productivity-around/

https://statista.com/outlook/372/100/online-dating/worldwide#market-globalRevenue

https://appypie.com/sean-rad-the-man-behind-tinder

https://datingsitesreviews.com/staticpages/index.php?page=Tinder-Statistics-Facts-History

https://vox.com/2018/5/19/17370288/silicon-valley-how-many-billionaires-start-up-tech-bay-area

https://wealthx.com/report/the-wealth-x-billionaire-census-2020/

Chapter 5—People

https://tonyrobbins.com/mind-meaning/the-mentors-who-coached-me/

https://tonyrobbins.com/news/tony-robbins-partnership-with-feeding-america-to-provide-one-billion-meals/

https://biography.com/business-figure/warren-buffett#higher-education

https://footwearnews.com/2019/business/retail/zappos-culture-retail-future-strategy-interview-1202777453/

Lacy, S. July 22, 2009. *Amazon Buys Zappos; The Price is $928m.*, not $847m. TechCrunch.

https://zappos.com/about/stories/zappos-20th-birthday

"10https://jayshetty.me/my-story/ Money Lessons from Billionaires." Ca.finance.yahoo.com. Retrieved 1 August 2018

https://page1.digital/blog/the-top-10-richest-social-media-entrepreneurs/

https://givingpledge.org/

Chapter 6—Partnerships

https://allbound.com/resource-center/successful-strategic-alliances-5-examples-of-companies-doing-it-right/

https://stimmel-law.com/en/articles/joint-ventures-compared-partnerships-single-purpose-partnership#:~:text=A%20joint%20venture%20involves%20two,to%20undertake%20a%20specific%20task.

https://pwc.com/us/en/services/deals/joint-ventures-strategic-alliances.html

https://stories.starbucks.com/press/2019/tata-starbucks-achieves-100-pay-equity/#:~:text=Starbucks%20entered%20the%20Indian%20market,2%2C000%20passionate%20partners%20(employees).

https://techinasia.com/talk/fail-china-lessons

Branson, R. 1998. *Losing My Virginity: How I've Survived, Had Fun, and Made a Fortune Doing Business My Way.*

https://virgin.com/virgingroup/content/about-us

https://businessinsider.com/virgin-group-richard-branson-net-worth-spending-2018-10?r=US&IR=T#to-branson-the-biggest-luxury-isnt-money-if-were-talking-about-personal-luxuries-and-the-luxury-of-being-your-own-boss-the-biggest-reward-is-the-amount-of-time-one-can-find-for-family-and-friends-38

"Richard Branson." *Forbes*

https://virgin.com/virgingroup/case-study-0

https://virgin.com/richard-branson/biography

"Bernard Ecclestone & Family." Forbes. Retrieved 8 November 2011, https://bleacherreport.com/articles/542560-f1s-billion-dollar-brain-a-short-history-of-bernie-ecclestone

https://formula1.com/en/latest/article.f1-broadcast-to-1-9-billion-fans-in-2019.4IeYkWSoexxSIeJyuTrk22.html

Chapter 7—Process

https://smartsheet.com/comprehensive-guide-values-principles-agile-manifesto

https://medium.com/@rashmisahu701/top-10-agile-companies-2018-42bbeb6368fd

https://scrumguides.org/scrum-guide.html

Moukheiber, Z. April 18, 2012. "Epic Systems' Tough Billionaire." *Forbes*. Retrieved 17 February 2019

https://forbes.com/sites/deloitte/2020/01/14/managing-global-tax-delivering-value-and-confidence/#659a76eb7293

https://forbes.com/profile/judy-faulkner/#7f22564833b8

https://investopedia.com/articles/markets/072016/netflix-7-secrets-you-didnt-know-nflx.asp#:~:text=Netflix%20CEO%20Reed%20Hastings%20came,company%20to%20fund%20the%20venture.

https://bloomberg.com/billionaires/profiles/reed-hastings/

https://onepercentfortheplanet.org/about

https://pricingforprofit.com/pricing-strategy-blog/are-all-songs-on-apple-s-itunes-priced-at-99.htm

https://rollingstone.com/culture/culture-news/itunes-10th-anniversary-how-steve-jobs-turned-the-industry-upside-down-68985/

https://startups.co.uk/pricing-strategies-price-skimming-penetration-pricing-and-premium-pricing/

https://europeanceo.com/lifestyle/apple-has-brought-itunes-to-an-end-let-the-streaming-wars-commen

https://bits.blogs.nytimes.com/2013/05/24/laurene-powell-jobs-and-anonymous-giving-in-silicon-valley/ce/

Chapter 8—Planet

http://socialinnovation.lv/wp-content/uploads/2015/07/Business-model-webam-small.pdf

https://abcnews.go.com/International/TenWays/story?id=3602269&page=1

https://encyclopedia.com/social-sciences-and-law/economics-business-and-labor/businesses-and-occupations/body-shop-international-plc

Sinclair, P. December 22, 2007. "Grameen Micro-Credit & How to End Poverty from the Roots Up." *One World One People*. Retrieved February 4, 2008. *Grameen Bank Historical Data*. Retrieved 22 June 2009.

Fraser, I. August 3, 2007. "Microfinance Comes of Age." Cover Story. Scottish Banker magazine. Archived from the original on 7 October 2007. Retrieved 30 January 2008.

Sydney Peace Prize recipients, Sydney Peace Prize Foundation website; Retrieved: 9 September 2007.

Byrne, J.A. April 9, 2012. "The 12 Greatest Entrepreneurs of our Time." *Fortune*. Archived from the Original on March 24, 2012.

https://upworthy.com/a-customer-walked-into-his-pizza-shop-and-changed-philadelphia-with-1-and-a-post-it-note

https://insidehook.com/article/food-and-drink/16-brands-use-toms-model-one-one-giving

https://brandsfortheheart.com/articles/99-mission-statements-examples-from-impact-brands-ideas-to-inspire-your-brands-higher-purpose/

https://bigissue.com/about/

https://forbes.com/sites/lilachbullock/2019/03/05/2019s-top-5-most-innovative-and-impactful-social-enterprises/#2412399a774a

http://grameen.com/

https://toms.co.uk/blakes-bio

About the Author

Marina Nicholas is a multi-award winning entrepreneur with a track record in helping companies identify and implement strategies to grow their business. Marina has spent over 25 years working with companies, from start-ups to large corporates, across sectors globally. An experienced board advisor with a passion to help people and companies thrive.

Marina's mission is to build a community of successful impact entrepreneurs passionate about helping humanity and the planet. Meet Marina at www.marinanicholas.com

Index

OTHER TITLES IN THE ENTREPRENEURSHIP AND SMALL BUSINESS MANAGEMENT COLLECTION

Scott Shane, Case Western University, Editor

- *Native American Entrepreneurs* by Ron P. Sheffield and Mark J. Munoz
- *Blockchain Value* by Olga V. Mack
- *TAP Into Your Potential* by Rick De La Guardia
- *Stop, Change, Grow* by Michael Carter and Karl Shaikh
- *From Starting Small to Winning Big* by Shishir Mishra
- *Dynastic Planning* by Walid S. Chiniara
- *How to Succeed as a Solo Consultant* by Stephen D. Field
- *Small Business Management* by Andreas Karaoulanis
- *Department of Startup* by Ivan Yong Wei Kit and Sam Lee
- *The Entrepreneurial Adventure* by David James and Oliver James
- *Cultivating an Entrepreneurial Mindset* by Tamiko L. Cuellar
- *On All Cylinders, Second Edition* by Ron Robinson
- *From Vision to Decision* by Dana K. Dwyer
- *Get on Board* by Olga V. Mack
- *The Rainmaker* by Jacques Magliolo
- *Family Business Governance* by Keanon J. Alderson

Announcing the Business Expert Press Digital Library

Concise e-books business students need for classroom and research

This book can also be purchased in an e-book collection by your library as

- a one-time purchase,
- that is owned forever,
- allows for simultaneous readers,
- has no restrictions on printing, and
- can be downloaded as PDFs from within the library community.

Our digital library collections are a great solution to beat the rising cost of textbooks. E-books can be loaded into their course management systems or onto students' e-book readers. The **Business Expert Press** digital libraries are very affordable, with no obligation to buy in future years. For more information, please visit **www.businessexpertpress.com/librarians**. To set up a trial in the United States, please email **sales@businessexpertpress.com**.

www.ingramcontent.com/pod-product-compliance
Lightning Source LLC
Chambersburg PA
CBHW061321220326
41599CB00026B/4976